Forgotten Victims
of Sex Abusers

Forgotten Victims of Sex Abusers

For Spouses, Families, Friends, and Parishioners

WILLIAM F. KRAFT

WIPF & STOCK · Eugene, Oregon

FORGOTTEN VICTIMS OF SEX ABUSERS
For Spouses, Families, Friends, and Parishioners

Copyright © 2020 William F. Kraft. All rights reserved. Except for brief quotations in critical publications or reviews, no part of this book may be reproduced in any manner without prior written permission from the publisher. Write: Permissions, Wipf and Stock Publishers, 199 W. 8th Ave., Suite 3, Eugene, OR 97401.

Wipf & Stock
An Imprint of Wipf and Stock Publishers
199 W. 8th Ave., Suite 3
Eugene, OR 97401

www.wipfandstock.com

PAPERBACK ISBN: 978-1-7252-5570-8
HARDCOVER ISBN: 978-1-7252-5571-5
EBOOK ISBN: 978-1-7252-5572-2

Manufactured in the U.S.A.   FEBRUARY 11, 2020

Especially for those who
loved or trusted a sex abuser

I thank the victims of sex abuse who shared their painful stories. Thanks are also offered to Heather, Jennifer, and Sharon for their personal and editorial help.

Contents

	Introduction	1
CHAPTER ONE	Forgotten Victims	3
CHAPTER TWO	The Abusers	16
CHAPTER THREE	Models of Abuse	27
CHAPTER FOUR	What is Sex Abuse?	31
CHAPTER FIVE	You Find Out	36
CHAPTER SIX	What to Avoid	45
CHAPTER SEVEN	Codependency	49
CHAPTER EIGHT	The Spiritual Power of Recovery	56
CHAPTER NINE	HABITS	59
CHAPTER TEN	Boundaries	67
CHAPTER ELEVEN	Detachment	70
CHAPTER TWELVE	Psychological Strategies	73
CHAPTER THIRTEEN	Communication	80
CHAPTER FOURTEEN	Forgiveness, Humility, and Gratitude	85
CHAPTER FIFTEEN	New Life	91
CHAPTER SIXTEEN	A Postscript to Sex Abusers	97
	Bibliography	101

Introduction

WE THANK THE COURAGEOUS victims who disclosed their abuse and helped us to understand how being a victim of sex is one of our most devastating and lasting experiences. They showed how sexual maltreatment is not only physical but also emotional, social, and spiritual defilement.

We are also grateful for judicial and media interventions that deepened our awareness of the prevalence and sacrilegious nature of sex abuse. The spotlight, and rightly so, has been on the intended victims of sex predators.

However, relatively less attention has been given to unintended victims who are often the most silent, invisible, and forgotten victims—spouses, families, friends, and parishioners who unknowingly knew a sex abuser. My intention is to listen to and remember people who trusted, often admired, and perhaps loved a person whom they later discovered was a sex offender.

We can ask ourselves what we might undergo if a family member, relative, or friend told us that he or she was sexually abused by a person (relative, friend, minister, et.al.) whom we trusted or welcomed in our personal life. Sadness, qualms, anger, or some kind of enduring pain would probably plague us.

We will reach out to women and their children who discover that their husband and daddy is found guilty of sexual assault. We will try to help parishioners, staff, and clergy who trusted, worked, and shared with pedophile priests and their enablers.

We will connect with women who find themselves disillusioned and in debt because of their husband's addiction to pornography or prostitutes, or both. We will also offer consolation and advice to committed women and men whose spouse is unfaithful. They too are victims.

Although such collateral victims are seldom the abuser's primary targets, they often suffer alone and with little help. I want to cease forgetting these victims and offer them help.

My thesis is that sex abusers cause severe and lasting harm to intended and unintended victims primarily because they violate spiritual bonds such as trust, fidelity, and love. Thus, healing and effective management not only involves medical and psychological but also spiritual assistance.

We begin with stories of inadvertent victims of sex abusers. We will listen to their thoughts and feelings and look at how they behaved. Chapter two gives the perspectives of their abusers. After these introductions, we reflect on the nature and dynamics of sex abusers, and how and why they victimize their loved ones. The rest of the book is about helping victims learn how to avoid and learn from mistakes and to practice effective ways to manage and heal. Let us begin.

Chapter One

Forgotten Victims

THE FOLLOWING VIGNETTES INTRODUCE us to families and friends who discovered that the person they trusted and often loved has been and is a sex/intimacy abuser. Some of their stories may resonate in you. My hope is that we garner some compassion for and understanding of these forgotten victims as well as listen to and learn from them.

Step in the shoes of Rita whose husband sexually pursued pubescent girls. "My God, never in my worst dreams did I think Phil would do or even could do what he did. Good God, he was having internet sex with young, adolescent girls; that's so sickening.

"And dummy me? I thought he was a faithful husband; he never abused me, or so I thought, until now. He was a good father, I think, to our two kids, was involved in our church and community, and everybody liked him. I never had an inkling of what he was doing until the police informed me that he was in jail.

"In short, a police woman posed over the internet as a fourteen year old girl who engaged in sex talk with my husband. They agreed to meet each other, and when he arrived to meet her, he was arrested.

"Since then, Phil contends that he never planned to have sex with a minor, but that he was only curious about her. When shown the internet transcripts of his filthy conversations, he admitted of getting out of bounds, but says that it wasn't real sex.

"Phil told his mother that it was all a misunderstanding, and that he simply made some mistakes that he regrets. Simply!? Mistakes!? He assured her that he is not a pedophile, that he would never harm a girl or cheat on his wife. Really!? Never harm!? Never cheat!? He pointed out to her that he's been a good worker and father as well as active in religious and social affairs.

"To say the least, my life changed so quickly and so much. I feel like I'm drowning in a flood of questions. How could such a grotesque thing happen without me sensing it? What do people think? Where did I go wrong? Will my kids be innocent victims and scarred for life. Where's Dad? Why is he in jail? How am I going to put our lives back together? Does anyone understand?

"I was mentioned in the news, but that's all. Nobody's heard my story. Nobody's reached out to me, except for my two best friends. They listen to and care about me. I thank God for them."

Listen to one of Phil's friends. "I don't know what to say. Surprised, stunned, and speechless are words that come to mind. I thought I knew him pretty well. Ha! He sure in hell fooled me—and, I feel like a fool. Disillusioned? You bet. And I'm angry, and sad.

"Good grief, he spent time in my house when my teenage daughter was there. In fact, a couple of times he took her swimming. What was he thinking? Was he lusting after her? Why didn't I pick up some signs? I liked and trusted the S.O.B. God, my friend is a sneaky and slimy pervert."

Here is what his pastor had to say. "Well, you know, I've heard practically everything; so, rarely does anything surprise or shock me. But! I have to admit that when I saw Phil on television, I was taken back.

"Look, Phil has been very active in our church. He spent considerable time and energy not only in fund raising and liturgical planning, but he also was a choir member, cantor, and overall leader. Come to think of it, he was active in youth ministry, and he even chaperoned on our camping and mission trips. I think most people, me included, trusted Phil."

Rita, her children, his mother, friend, and pastor are victims of Phil's sex offenses, albeit not in the same way as his intended victims, the adolescent girls he lured with sex talk. All of these unintended victims trusted and admired him, and some loved him. No one was aware of Phil's duplicitous life. They were fooled, manipulated, and violated.

In time, Rita will be forgotten or remembered as the woman with the pedophile husband. Some people might shun her and her children, and may even make them targets of ridicule. Still others may offer them compassionate help. Whatever happens to them, their wounds of victimization will radically change their lives.

Phil's mother and father, siblings, friends, pastor, and co-workers are also victims. They too are disillusioned and baffled, but differently than Rita, the children, and the targeted victims—the adolescent girls. Indeed, one person can seriously wound many people.

It's shocking to discover that the person you loved and trusted is so different. Our first reaction is often disbelief and/or denial. Like Phil's wife and his mother, you may feel that it couldn't be this bad, or there must be some mistake, or I'll wake up from this nightmare. This cannot be! "I can't believe it" is a common refrain.

Like Rita, when we find out that someone we trusted has deceived and manipulated us, and indulged in sick, immoral, and criminal sex, we too would probably be dazed, frozen, and numb—in shock. We too may want to scream, and yet be speechless. We too may want to do something, but feel stuck. We too may feel queasy, nauseous, and simply sick. Suddenly our world has changed. Although we were not the targets of his addiction, we are among his victims.

Dictionaries define a victim as someone who is injured, destroyed, or killed. If you have been in a situation like Rita's, you were probably not a planned target of abuse; nevertheless, you have been and are seriously injured. Your life, as you have been living it, won't be the same, and how it will be, you don't know. Although the sex abuser probably did not intend to victimize you, you are a victim.

Indeed, you have been cut off from what you thought was true and based your life on. Especially if you were close to the abuser, like Rita, your bonds of trust and love have been severed. We can see that sex abuse is not only physical and psychological, but also it is spiritual in that it violates what and whom you trusted and often held sacred. No wonder you feel the way you do.

Listen to Alice who is a victim of a common type of sex abuse—pornography and extra-marital sex. "How would you feel if you discovered that your husband of 15 years and father of three children spent his time, energy, and our money on porn, strip clubs, massage parlors, and prostitutes? I couldn't believe it.

"How could he spend our savings, the kids' college funds, take out a second mortgage, and avoid paying some bills, including the taxes? It sounds impossible, but it happened. How could anyone be so self-centered and selfish? And for what? Sick sex?

"You might wonder why it took so long for me to find out. Well, dummy me, I trusted him not only with our finances, but also with my heart. I trusted and thought I loved this imposter, liar, pervert, my husband. It's nauseating and pathetic. I feel so used, so violated, so betrayed.

"Zack thinks it's not such a big deal. Well, it changed my life, forever. He says he's sorry and I should forgive, forget, and get on with life. He says that he's never given his heart to any woman except me. To say the least, this frustrates and angers me.

"When I go ballistic, he points to my behavior as proof of my problems. In spite of the overwhelming evidence of his betrayal, I end up being the problem. He certainly knows how to push my buttons. What can I do to make him get it? Will he ever understand?

"The relentless questions of what if and if only badger me. Why, why, why get no comforting answers. A good night's sleep is rare. Stomach and heart aches, anger, anxiety, depression, and fear plague me. Yes, I know I'm drinking too much, but it takes the edge off, at least for a while.

"Sometimes I feel so beaten and weary that I wonder if I'll make it through the day. I don't know what the future holds for me. Yet, something or someone within me says that I can and will make it. Time will tell."

Alice is a seldom recognized victim of sex abuse. Yet, she manifests symptoms of a post- traumatic stress disorder. Recurrent and distressing thoughts and feelings about her husband's behavior haunt her. Nightmares and obsessive thinking disturb her sleep. She suffers from gastrointestinal ailments, is emotionally labile and hyper-vigilant, obsesses about her husband, drinks too much, and feels detached from others, and overall, not well. Meanwhile, Zack seems to suffer relatively little.

Think of Alice in regards to her children, marriage, and future. Being a single mother, a sole homemaker, and a full-time worker is one of the most stressful ways to live. And remember, Zack will always be the children's father, no matter what he does.

Whether Alice remains married or gets divorced, she can learn to deal with her husband or ex with less stress and more effectiveness. Instead of letting him push her buttons, she can learn to change her steps in this toxic dance. For instance, she can learn to avoid co-dependent thinking and reactions, set healthy boundaries, connect with helpful people, and bond with her interior sources of empowerment and healing. In short, we will show how she can cope more effectively, heal, and come to a better life.

Here is another person, Faith, who trusted and loved her husband, and discovered that her husband has been sexually involved with men.

"It's bad enough to find out that your husband pleasured himself with porn, or that he had sex with other women. But, when the pornography and affairs are with men, that's a different story.

"After seventeen years of marriage and two children, I hear the never ending echoes in my mind. Guess what, Faith, your husband, Joseph, craves sex with men. What does that make me?

Was I second best? Was I simply a baby maker, caretaker, and homemaker?

"Were his affection and sex merely ways to appease and deceive me? Did he think about men when he was making so-called love with me? Did he fantasize about men to get aroused with me?

"Indeed, we had some but not serious problems, so I thought. Moreover, I always assumed that he was committed, faithful, and desired me. Besides, Joseph has been a good provider and a better than average father to our two girls. So, from a distance, we looked like a good family and couple.

"Where was I? Why did it take me so long to find out that I've been married to a gay guy? How could I've been so dumb? Why didn't I suspect something? Why didn't I question his late nights and weekend work schedule? What a chump I've been.

"I trusted this man. Where was his concern for me? Did he ever think that he could have infected me with a sexually transmitted disease? It was and is all about him.

"Ironically, I've been a gay rights advocate. Although I'm not sure if gay marriage should be a sacrament, I do think that homosexuals should at least be accepted, valued, and treated fairly. I know that my husband didn't choose his sexual orientation, but he did choose to marry me and to be sexually active with men. That's wrong!"

Like all victims of sex/intimacy offenses, Faith has to deal with the psychological (functional) and spiritual (intimacy) violations. Her husband is not a criminal or mentally ill. She knows that his intent was not to hurt her, but he did. Moreover, no one, except herself, may know of her plight. She is an invisible and silent victim.

As with most victims, Faith's life has radically changed. She finds herself questioning her own sexuality and judgment as well as wrestling with what is best for her and her children's futures. Should she stay in the marriage for financial and parental reasons? Should and can she learn to tolerate a functional relationship without intimacy? Should and can she look good in public, and suffer in private? Or can and should she start a new life?

Our intent is not to imply that homosexuality is an illness, but that infidelity, homo- or hetero- sexual, seriously violates trust and desecrates a relationship. Moreover, when one marries under false pretenses, the consequences are devastating to the person of good faith. The honest person, like Faith, is an unintended victim.

Will Faith ever regain her trust not just with men, but also with life, God, and herself? Will she ever rekindle her self-respect and feel good about being a woman? Will she recover and regain her well-being? Will she ever look in a mirror and smile? Yes, perhaps with tears.

Consider how Eleanor deals with a relatively unusual type of sex abuse. "I've learned to live with it. After all, for the 35 years of our marriage, Jude has been an excellent provider and a good father to our four children. He has always treated me with respect, albeit our life of intimacy was and is not good.

"So, what have I learned to live with? Well, he calls it a predilection, and I've learned to call it that as well. Technically, you could say Jude is a masochist who needs women to inflict pain on him. Simply stated, Jude gets intense sexual pleasure when a woman insults, degrades, and physically hurts him. Once or twice a month, Jude visits a woman who gives him, for a fee, what he wants.

"From the beginning of our marriage, Jude wanted me to play sex games wherein I would mock and scourge him. I tried to play the part, but I just couldn't see how this helped our relationship. I simply didn't feel good about it. So I stopped doing it.

"After six years of marriage, three children, and another on the way, I found out about his extra-marital behavior, paying prostitutes to satisfy his masochistic needs. For a time that seemed like an eternity, I was confused, embarrassed, angry, scared, depressed; you name it, and I felt it. So, why did I stay with Jude?

"Well, as I have already noted, he's been a good father, worker, provider, and community organizer as well as active in our church. So, I weighed the pros and cons, and wondered whether, at my age, I could do any better. Indeed, money has given our kids and me wonderful opportunities.

"In short, Jude and I have a civil relationship, and I've learned to live without physical intimacy. I suppose you could call me a married celibate. I compensate with friendships, cultural events, and travel. To me, my prayer life along with church activities and daily worship have especially helped me to keep my honor. Sure, my life could be better, but it's not so bad."

Not many people find themselves in Eleanor's situation, but we may share more common ground with her than we initially think. Consider when your needs of security, love, and opportunity are in jeopardy. How do you feel? What would you do? No decision is perfect. So, what is the best imperfect decision? When you discern the positives and negatives, what do you decide?

Eleanor is a victim. She entered her marriage with good will and commitment. Unlike her husband, she has been a faithful and good spouse. Her bond of sexual love with her husband has been severely debased. She could easily get a civil divorce and a religious annulment. You could argue that Eleanor's husband is sick and needs help, or at least is unfair, and criticize her for enabling her husband's behavior.

Yet, with considerable, ambivalent thought, she chose to remain with her husband. Why? Indeed, Eleanor does enable her husband to hurt her and to violate her marital bonds of love. However, besides dire consequences, her decision also enables positive opportunities for herself and her children. Thus, she enables both negative and positive consequences. In short, with discernment, Eleanor decided to stay in her marriage because she thinks it is the best imperfect decision for herself and her children.

With the help of a counselor and friends, Eleanor learned to depend on family, friends, and God, and not on her husband for her happiness. She has learned how to tolerate and cope with her husband's so-called predilection, at times with compassion. She harbors little resentment and anger, and maintains her dignity and serenity. Moreover, she has learned to compensate for her losses with recreational, cultural, and spiritual gains. Clearly, you could make a very different choice than Eleanor, and both of you could be right.

Let us reflect on how sex violence can harm and victimize relative strangers or a group of people, such as a church parishioners. Listen to Martha, a religiously committed woman who was very active in her church.

"God, religion, and church were always important to me. So, when I saw our pastor on the evening news being taken to jail on charges of pedophilia, I was stunned.

"Three men accused our pastor of past sexual abuse. One of the alleged abuses apparently occurred as recently as two years ago, and another happened more than twenty. The abuses had one thing in common: They were done with teenage boys.

"Needless to say, the parish was humming with chatter, opinions, and theories. Most of us were in disbelief, for we thought Father Ron was a good pastor. He gave fine homilies, celebrated liturgy with reverence, had excellent pastoral skills, and was financially adept. Sex offender did not fit our picture of our pastor.

"The media portrayed him as a despicable pedophile, and in the end the jury found him guilty of sex offenses against minors. He is currently serving a 10-year prison sentence. Our bishop apologized for his grave sin and insured us that Rev. Ron would never be in active ministry.

"We, the people, had many reactions. Many of us were disillusioned and angry. We felt that our pastor duped and manipulated us. This man, whom we trusted, followed, supported, and honored, turned out to be a monster. Yes, he was a wolf in sheep's clothing,

"We thought that the church was a sacred and safe place where we could rest securely, share with trust, find consolation, and be led to God. Now, we're not so sure. I feel betrayed, and I'm not alone in how I feel. Some of my friends in anger and distrust are leaving the church.

"Look, I'm angry too. I trusted not only my pastor but also his bishops who enabled him. I look at these so-called holy leaders still living plush lives with little or no consequences for their sinful and criminal behavior. Instead, they use our money to pay their legal fees to protect themselves.

"I've endured their generic programs to protect God's children. It seems to me that they protect themselves more than children. Any so-called changes did not come from their initiatives, but from media and legal pressure. Tell me, what systematic changes have they made? Not much has really changed. They say the words, but they don't walk their talk. How many of these holy leaders have entered and work a recovery program? They wouldn't stoop so low. Please, cut me a break.

"I think I get some glimpses of how victims feel. Think of being a young person who is naïve, trustworthy, and innocent. Think of a boy, or girl, who looks up to a priest, trusts and admires him, sees him as a representative of Christ, and calls him Father. Think of how dependent and vulnerable he is. Think of how the priest used his power to wound this youngster forever.

"Think of how the lives of these boys were shattered not only because of the sexual abuse but also because their relationships with the church, religion, and God are changed forever. Think of the boys' families and how they entrusted their sons to Father. Think of how violated and diminished they must feel. Who really responds to their profound and enduring pain?"

Martha harbors anger and resentment, for she feels duped and betrayed. She feels that some bishops are concerned more for their institution and status than for the welfare of the youthful victims. Martha is not the same kind of victim as the young teenagers whom Rev. Ron violated, nor the same as the loved ones of the victims and of Father Ron; nevertheless, she and other parishioners are victims.

With compassion and insight her heart reaches out to the victims who suffer from clergy abuse. She tries to put herself in the shoes of the victims and their parents, and prays for and reaches out to them.

Martha has not left her church, for she strongly thinks that the church belongs to her as much as to the ordained. She says she is not going to wait for the leaders to lead, but she and others are committed to speak out, respectfully demand changes, and act. Forgiveness? Mercy? Martha says that they are works in progress.

Indeed, when you care for or trust someone, what they do affects you. Think about these parents whose adult child is a sex abuser. "My wife and I are at our wits end about what to do about our daughter. We don't know what has happened to her. So, here's the story in a nutshell.

"As a child, teenager, and young adult, Karen was picture perfect. Unlike her older sister, she never gave us problems. Karen graduated summa cum laude from college, and went on to earn graduate degrees in mathematics and computer science. She quickly got a high paying job and performed extremely well. Our only concern was that she was all work and no play.

"Then seemingly out of the clear blue sky, she informed us that she was entering the religious life to become a nun. Although we had misgivings, we supported her.

Actually, the religious life helped her to loosen up and became more outgoing. She seemed to blossom and to be more balanced. However, when she was due to take permanent vows, she surprised us again, and decided to leave after nine years in her community.

"Soon after she left, all hell broke loose in that she became very promiscuous. She seemed to go to the opposite extreme of her old prim and proper self. Karen would go with a guy for a couple of weeks at best and often just for one night. Her need for sex seemed insatiable. Initially, we thought she may have been on drugs or drinking too much, but she really wasn't.

"When we questioned her, she firmly stated that it was her business. We expressed our concern for her safety, that she could contract a disease or encounter a violent man. She assured us that she could take care of herself, while we watched her destroying herself. We couldn't stop her, though we wanted to. Where did that perfect girl with so much sense go? Really, she was like an addict who needed a fix.

"Her sister is furious with Karen, and confronts her irresponsibility. She simply tells her that it is about time to grow up and get a life. I doubt if Mary's approach is effective, but it's her way.

"Karen's novice director and her other formators were saddened but not surprised to hear of Karen's sexual escapades. Although these religious sisters always thought Karen was very intelligent and gifted, they also thought that she was too cerebral and affectively constricted. They helped Karen to loosen her tight grip and express her emotions.

"Ironically, the freedom she found in the religious life was transformed into a license for sexual promiscuity. At least, that's the way we see it. I guess we'd like to put the young, the religious, and the present Karen into a blender so that she would come out as an intelligent, responsible, religious, and passionate woman.

"However, as the nuns told us, we cannot nor should we try to fix Karen. They advised us to love Karen as she is, and not to get in God's way."

Indeed, such sexual indiscretions also affect parents, siblings, and other loved ones. Although the broken bonds are somewhat different than in a marriage, they nevertheless cause disruption and pain to those who care. To feel helpless in watching your child endanger and hurt herself is heart wrenching. Such parents are unintended victims, even though people may not frame it this way.

One might speculate that in adolescence and young adulthood, Karen repressed her emotions and accrued a slush fund of affectivity. In religious life, her affective dam began to show cracks and leaks. When she returned to lay life as a new woman, her dam broke and flooded her life with passion and sex.

Is Karen a sex abuser? She probably qualifies because she craves sex and has lost control; she obsesses about and is compelled to have sex. She is not as free as she can or would like to be. Moreover, Karen jeopardizes herself, and rationalizes the negative consequences to herself and family. Although it is not her intent, her sexual behavior victimizes her parents and sister, and probably others who care for her.

We have listened to overlooked victims who include spouses, children, siblings, parents, friends, neighbors, pastors, and parishioners. These unintended victims are ordinary people who must deal with their pain often without much recognition and help. To shed more light on this darkness, we will present the retorts of the sex abusers who have hurt the people who care for them. We can listen to what victimizers have to say, and perhaps increase our understanding.

Chapter Two

The Abusers

IN THIS CHAPTER, we give the abusers in the previous chapter an opportunity to speak, to give them a forum to explain themselves. A caveat: What you hear may be upsetting.

To be sure, our purpose is not to defend or justify abusers. Rather, our intent is to understand them and thereby learn to manage and feel better. We will see that sex abusers often share behavioral profiles.

For example, many sex abusers (and some of their friends) initially minimize how much they have hurt you, the unintended victim. One reason is that unlike you, sex abusers usually separate sex (body) and love (spirit). They see sex as simply pleasure and not intimacy that calls for love. The repeated refrain of victims: "They just don't get it," is usually true.

Another common coping of abusers is to steer the focus away from themselves, and focus on you. Initially, most abusers deny, lie about, rationalize, or give only parts of their story. Some admit to "making some mistakes" and promise to change. A few defend their behavior, or blame you as the cause of their "understandable" misbehavior. Once again, you are abused.

In our first vignette, most people would call Phil a pedophile. (Technically, Phil is an ephebophile—one who desires sexual intimacy with young adolescents.) Let us listen to what Phil has to say.

"If you would have told me five years ago that I would do serious prison time for being a sex offender, I'd have said that you're out of your mind. I was married to a wonderful woman, had two adult children who also loved me dearly, had a great job, and was known and respected in the community.

"Now, I can't get a decent job, I'm on a public list of sex offenders, my wife divorced me, and my kids are leery of me, I'm limited to where I live and work, have a felony, friends have disappeared, and so on. Most people see me as a criminal, sinner, and/or sick. And, they're right. So, what happened?

"The following may sound like an excuse, and it may be, but this is what happened. I had a job that eventually gave me plenty of free time, which I began to fill with adult porn—sinful but not a crime. In a matter of months, I spent four or more hours per day and more on weekends with porn. Then I got into chat rooms, and even met a few women.

"I got bored or crazy, and slid into adolescent porn. I told myself I was just curious, and started sexting with some teenagers. I eventually made a date with a girl at a fast food restaurant, again rationalizing that I was curious and would never have sex with a young girl. Well, you know the rest of the story; police were waiting for me.

"Would I have had sex with a pubescent girl? I say no. But, am I fooling myself? How low would I go? I know now that I was on a slippery and slimy slope where anything was possible and nothing fulfilling. I needed more and more, and it was never enough.

"I ruined my life as well as those who loved and trusted me. Believe me, this was not my intent. Nevertheless, I sought sexual excitement without regard for their welfare. In two years, I wiped out a good life.

"I rarely have the desire for porn now, but I know that demons hide but seldom die. I work my Sexaholics Anonymous program and try to make amends. I'm not sure what the future holds for me."

Pornography of whatever kind is an awfully lucrative business—and, it is addictive. Unlike Phil, most porn addicts do not regress into adolescent (or child) pornography, but some do. So, why did Phil fall into criminal activity? Nobody can say with certainty what moved Phil to do what he did, but here are some thoughts.

Phil was not the so-called dirty old man who lived on the other side of the tracks. He was successful and well known in social, church, and community activities. He felt on top of the world, and perhaps that was part of his problem.

Phil lacked humility. He felt that he could do and get away with anything, while not caring about hurting anyone. His primary fault was not sexual desire and satisfaction, but more so a grandiose sense of power. As many sex addicts say, I did it because I could do it.

Phil became increasingly obsessed with "more and more," chasing the elusive high that would finally be enough. In some respects, Phil is similar to a drug addict, though his sex abuse is more interpersonally intimate than substance abuse.

My intent is not to use addiction as an excuse or to minimize the horrific reality of sex with adolescents and children. My point is that addiction takes physiological, psychosocial, and spiritual control of the offender. Sex addiction incessantly lures and pressures the abuser to act in ways that are criminal, sick, and sinful.

Not only Phil, but his ex-wife, children, parents, and friends will never be the same. They carry scars that he inflicted on them. This book is about how to make those wounds count so that they help you, the victim, become a stronger and healthier person.

Remember our vignette of Alice, whose husband spent a lot of money on "legal" porn, sex clubs, massages, and prostitutes. Unlike Phil, Zack neither pursued illegal nor quite as destructive sex. Nevertheless, his behavior was very harmful to his loved ones as well as to himself. Listen to Zack's version of the story.

"Look, I admit I'm not perfect. Who is? Most guys look at porn, go to clubs, and when they can, have a little sex. I can understand why my wife's not pleased, but why is she so angry? I wasn't unfaithful. I didn't love any of those women. There was nothing personal.

"Okay, I admit I spent too much time and money, and that things got out of hand. I promised Alice that I'd pay off the debts, but I can't pay our debts as long as she insists on controlling the money. I'd have figured a way out.

"But, she says she doesn't trust me, so what am I supposed to do? If she wants to act that way, then that's on her. Anyway, to please her, I joined one of those twelve step groups, got their book, and for three months, I attended two meetings per week. What more does she want?

"I've done everything my wife wanted me to do, like joining a recovery group, giving her control of the money, and sleeping in a different bedroom. I even try to do extra chores around the house. Why can't she understand and forgive me so that we can get on with life. Can't she accept that I've gotten over my so-called problems? What's wrong with her?"

Clearly, Zack shows little understanding of and compassion for his wife. True contrition, amends, and recovery are conspicuously absent. Although Zack did not get sexually involved with minors, in some respects he is in worse shape than Phil who works a program of recovery, shows remorse, and tries to make amends.

With reluctance, Zack joined Sex and Love Anonymous and gave up control of the finances. His good will, however, seemed to be more compliance than a heartfelt commitment.

Zack needs to realize that he victimized his wife, that he violated and demeaned her. He gave little concern of how his sex activities would affect his loved ones. Like many men, Zack assumed that his so-called private sex life had no relation to love, and he still feels this way. He has to learn to show true remorse, stop complaining and blaming, face his shortcomings, and make personal and financial amends.

Let us listen to Joseph who lived a covert homosexual life while in a heterosexual marriage. "I never felt good about the double life I've led; I've always felt guilty and ashamed. Actually, it's driven me crazy.

"Just the logistics, cover-ups, and lying have been mind boggling and shameful. More importantly, I've been unfaithful and have betrayed a good woman, my wife, Faith. I certainly wouldn't recommend my life style to my children, or to anyone.

"You might ask, why haven't I changed my ways? I've tried. I got counseling, and I would avoid the gay life for a while. But, eventually, I'd return to it. The desire for gay contact was like a magnetic force that eventually drew me to it.

"My counselor encouraged me to join Sexaholics Anonymous, and I went to meetings, but I just didn't feel comfortable. I felt embarrassed, although there were guys just like me. It seems that the more I fought my desires for men, the stronger they became. To be honest, I don't know if I can give up the gay life.

"I truly love my wife and children. I feel crummy when fantasies about men appear while making love with Faith. Although I love her dearly, I prefer sex with a man. I wish I could be straight; it certainly would be easier and better, at least for my marriage.

"Since Faith found out about my secret life, I'm not sure what's going to happen. I don't want a divorce, but I understand why she would want one. I don't want to lose her and my children. I'm willing to do anything, including more counseling and S.A. I'm not sure what the future holds, and I'm scared to death."

This situation is not as uncommon as one might think. When men or women lead such a double life, their marriage and family will suffer. And, Joseph admits that his duplicitous life has done grave harm to both his wife and himself.

It's safe to say that Joseph did not choose his homosexual orientation, and that he loves his wife and children. The thought of losing them petrifies him. Nevertheless, he unintentionally victimized them. But as Faith said, he intentionally choose to marry her.

Is homosexuality a psychological disorder? Most mental health specialists would say that homosexuality is not unhealthy.

Most religious leaders would say that being homosexual is acceptable, but its genital expression is sinful.

Our view is that homosexuality is not a mental disorder. However, when one's homo- or hetero- sexual behavior is lustful, gets out of control, and harms oneself and others, it is not healthy and is abusive.

Recall, Jude, the successful and married man who desires sexual abuse. "I prefer to call my sexual preferences somewhat unique. Look, I keep my sexual predilections private so they don't upset my loved ones, especially my wife and kids. I really do love them, and I think I take good care of them.

"Moreover, I'm well known in the community and church as a leader and organizer. I have raised millions of dollars for charity. Without my different sexual satisfaction, I don't think I'd function as well as I do.

"I know that most people would judge my sexual behavior as peculiar or even pathological, and say that I need help. Well, I disagree with them. Admittedly, I think it's unfair to my wife, but my condition is not something I've chosen, and most people would say that do I a lot of good for others.

"Anyway, I've been honest with Eleanor, and I try to treat her well. She seems to have accepted our situation, and doesn't complain much. I really appreciate her good will and efforts to get along with me. She's a good woman. So, I guess that we'll continue to live the life that we've lived for the last 35 years."

Many people would claim that this man practices sick sex and needs help, or that he is a narcissistic manipulator. Others might argue that since he functions well and does considerable good, he is not sick or self-centered. From a religious/moral perspective, Jude is a sinner at least insofar as he has sex outside of his marriage.

Indeed, Jude is a successful entrepreneur as well as an esteemed member of his community and church. His monetary contributions do a lot of good. So, is Jude bad, sick, or simply different? Is his wife an enabler? Should she have divorced him? Or did she make a valid decision? What do you think?

Taking a holistic approach, one could argue that when we use functionality devoid of spirituality as the measure of health, we could argue that Jude is not sick. However, if we include the spiritual in our models for good and healthy living, Jude is less than whole or healthy.

The spotlight has been on the Roman Catholic Church and its clergy who have abused adolescents and on their enablers. Let's listen to Father Ron who sexually/spiritually abused male adolescents.

"Here I am in prison in a special unit to protect me from the other prisoners. Even criminals see me as the lowest of the low. And you know, they're probably right. I feel, as my mother used to call some bad people, like a slime ball. I plead guilty.

"Speaking of my mother, how do you think of she feels? One day she was proud of her son, the very educated, successful, and admired priest, and she thanked God every day for my vocation. And the next day, she saw me on television being hauled to jail in handcuffs for being a child molester. To say the least she was stunned, overwhelmed, confused. This simple, holy woman, my Mom, still suffers profoundly.

"She went from a humbly proud pillar of faith to a humiliated puddle of shame. Ditto for my older brother and sisters. Now people subtly stare and avoid them not for anything they did, but for what I did. Thank God my Dad is dead and doesn't have to bear the shame.

"What about the boys whom I manipulated and used, whose spirit I deflated, whose faith in religion and God I practically destroyed? They and their families trusted me. I emotionally and spiritually stained them for life. Can they or even should they forgive me?

"Why? I don't know. I got some therapy in prison, and since I've served my sentence, I got more. Why did I commit one of the worst sins and heinous crimes? Why did I devastate so many people? Why did I betray people who loved me, who trusted me, who honored me? Why did I abuse innocent, trusting, and vulnerable boys?

"I started to be aware of my sexual attraction for male adolescents in the seminary. I liked women, but not sexually. Of course, I didn't share any of this with anyone, especially my teachers and superiors. I was too afraid I'd be kicked out of the seminary.

"When ordained, a new world opened to me, one where people looked up to me, trusted me, confessed their sins to me, followed my advice. Who else but priests gets so much adoration, privilege, opportunity, and power? I was a master at practicing clericalism. As long as I kept out of trouble, I could do almost anything I wanted—or, so I thought.

"One of my responsibilities was to be in charge of youth ministry because, I suppose, I was young, no one else wanted the job, and I was good at it. Well, I found myself taking a special interest in shy, forgotten, and invisible adolescents, I guess because I saw myself in them when I was their age.

"Anyhow, I invited them into the worlds of sports, culture, travel, dinning, liturgy, charitable work—experiences they never had. We enjoyed and had fun with each other, and I might add, the parents were happy too. With gratitude, they called me Father.

"Well, I got closer and closer from a pat on the back to on the bum, to a hug, to a back rub, to linger on his loin, to a quick kiss on his lips, to a touch on his genitals, to unbuttoning his pants, and on and on. I assured him that although God blessed our intimacy, his parents would not understand. So, for God's sake, it would not be good to share this with anyone. That was my M.O.

"After many years of abusing adolescent boys, parents of one of my victims suspected something, and talked to the bishop about it. He assured both them that he would attend to the matter, and weeks later I was transferred to another parish. And of course after a period of fear and abstinence, I started all over again. An Addiction? Crime? Sin? Probably all three and more.

"Some time after the Boston exposé on priest pedophilia, our new bishop met with me to inform me of several allegations against me. Of course, I denied it. Following the new rules of the protecting God's children program, my bishop informed me that he would call the district attorney and let his people handle it. The bishop then suspended my priest faculties.

"The D.A.'s evidence was overwhelming, and I fessed up. I was taken to jail, and later was on probation until my trail. I was found guilty, and sentenced to ten years in prison.

"Now, I wonder how I am I going to live the rest of my life. I hope I can at least be good and grateful for my loved ones who stuck by me, and to make amends to them. Most important, besides prayer, I have to make some kind of amends to my adolescent victims. God help me."

There have been many priest pedophiles, and hopefully there will be far fewer or none. Indeed not many people are happy with the Roman Catholic Church. Though their trust has diminished, they still have hope and are willing to work to resurrect their Church.

In some respects, Father Ron is a better person and priest than he has ever been. He seems to feel shame, guilt, powerlessness, insight, and relatively genuine care. His clericalism has been decimated, and his spiritual life is better. He seems to be honestly contrite and humble.

Although Rev. Ron is paying a huge price for his heinous crimes, it is not nearly as great as that of his victims. His conversion, if it is true and continues, could lead to some ways of making amends. At least, he can pray for his victims, and mourn their losses.

Clergy and lay people contend that significant changes to protect young persons have been made and continue to be made. Moreover, financial and therapeutic help have been and are offered to intended victims.

Many unintended victims simply shrug their shoulders and say that clerical leaders will do what they want. Like Martha, they remain in their church to worship their God, and some act to change their church. Still others in sad and angry protest leave the church or give significantly less financial and communal support.

Let us visit Karen who left the religious life and became promiscuous. Although men are more likely than women to be more frequent sex abusers, women can also be sex and therefore spiritual abusers. However, most women, like Karen, are usually in a different place than men on the spectrum of sex abuse.

Here is Karen's story as she tells it. "Do you think I'm stupid? Of course, I know that I've been acting very differently than any other time in my life, and that I'm upsetting my parents and sister. I understand why they worry about me, but what's new—they've always had me under their microscope. Look, I know they love me, and that they mean well. But please, let me alone.

"Thank God for my religious sisters. I'll be eternally grateful to them, for they helped me escape my prison of emotionless perfectionism. Finally, I stopped living out of my mind, and got in touch with my feelings.

"I admit that my sexual behavior has been extreme, or promiscuous. I know I'm upsetting practically everyone, including God. I know that Ms. Perfect is very imperfect. But, therein lies the sense in the nonsense. It feels so good to be so bad.

"I realize that my sexual frenzy isn't healthy. It's as if I'm satisfying sexual desires of a 36 year-old woman with the maturity of a pubescent girl.

"I'm not proud of having one night or one hour stands, or hooking up with married men. Yet it seems as if my hormones have a mind of their own, like I'm almost compelled to have sex.

"Furthermore, there's more to it than mere sex. As you can see, I'm not very attractive. When a man wants me, albeit just for sex, I feel more worthwhile, more feminine, and more desirable. I know my behavior is ultimately futile, but it feels so much better than nothing.

"Admittedly, my craziness will soon run its course. Until then, I'm going to have some fun. Who knows, maybe my sinful, sexual behavior is preparing me for a virtuous life of love. Yet, now my life is moving more toward hell than heaven. So, I have nowhere to go but up."

Karen is an intelligent and insightful woman who knows that her compulsion to have sex is less than healthy, albeit it feels better than nothing. She knows that she is living the opposite extreme of her past, heady self. For the time being, sex/emotion rather than her past mind/cognition is her elixir.

Karen realizes that her promiscuous sex, or sex without love, will eventually end, for it fails to give her what she needs and wants. What she needs is to let go of her past resentment, improve her body image, be free from her perfectionism, and reconnect with her spiritual values and her God.

Karen also realizes that she upsets her family, though this is not her intent. Compounding matters is that some people may take pleasure in criticizing Karen and her family as holy hypocrites. In short, Karen's parents, sister, and friends suffer because of her sexual behavior. They are unintended victims.

Although Karen's behavior hurts and troubles her family, they are not shunning or condemning her. They're not giving up on her, but rather they wait with hope that she become her whole self.

We can begin to see that there is a wide spectrum of sex abusers. They share common features, and they differ in kind and degree of harm they inflict. To be sure, all sex abuses are less than healthy, are not good, some are criminal, and all have intended and unintended victims.

Chapter Three

Models of Abuse

A BASIC TENET IS that how we view and think about sex abuse highly influences our feelings, judgments, and responses to sex abuse. With this principle in mind, let us reflect on three common ways to understand and respond to questionable sexual behavior. Hopefully, these examples help us to refine our own assumptions and thoughts.

One approach is a "moral" one where we see sexual abuses as sins that need to be confessed and forgiven. In short, the sinner/abuser admits his sins/offences against his victims and God, promises to try not to commit them again, receives absolution, and feels back on the right track.

In contrast, we can take a "legal" approach, and judge certain sex behaviors as crimes that deserve punishment, while others are not crimes. For example, compulsive use of adult pornography is not a crime, though from a moral perspective, it is a sin. However, to consume child pornography is not only a sin but also a felony that usually results in imprisonment and public exposure.

Along with or instead of moral and legal approaches, we can subscribe to a "mental health" model. We think that because of their mental illness, certain sex abusers do not freely choose their behavior, but rather have a health disorder or disease that needs treatment. For example, a compulsively promiscuous person, who is a sinner but not a criminal, may enter a treatment facility to recover from his disorder.

Think of Karen, the promiscuous ex nun in chapter two. She can go to confession where the priest absolves her of sins, gives her a penance, and expects a firm purpose of amendment. From a legal perspective, she has not committed a crime, and therefore will not be given any consequences.

If Karen went to a mental health clinic, she may not be diagnosed as mentally ill, and more likely be offered help for underlying issues such as perfectionism, low self-esteem, and anxiety. So, we have three professionals taking different approaches toward the same behavior.

From these common perspectives, let us look at Andrew who married Sara. "I plead guilty. People told me that I was out of my mind to marry sweet, seductive Sara. They warned me about her promiscuous history and how she would use men. Guess what, I didn't heed their advice. I admit I was wrong, stupid, naïve, blind, stubborn—and, romantically in love with wonderfully crazy and fun-loving Sara.

"Before we were married, Sara told me that she wasn't proud of her past sexual escapades, but partly defended them because they advanced her professionally. She claimed that she had sex usually when she drank too much—and, she swore that she would change.

"I not only thought she'd keep her promise, but I also assumed that my love and financial resources would make her happy and faithful. I felt that if I loved, accepted, and understood her unconditionally, she would change her ways. Ha! Of course, Sara soon fell into her promiscuity.

"Well, I plead guilty to benevolent arrogance. With sincere intentions, I thought my love would change her, that I was that powerful. Good God, even Jesus Christ never changed people without their cooperation."

Models of Abuse

The situation of Andrew and Sara is not uncommon. They are not criminals. From a moral/religious perspective, Both Sara (fornication, infidelity) and Andrew (benevolent arrogance and pride) could be judged as sinful and needing reconciliation.

Mental health providers might say that Sara is a troubled and sad woman who needs help with issues like shame and intimacy. They might see Andrew as a co-dependent man who needs to learn how to detach, set boundaries, and find his worth within himself. In short, neither Andrew nor Sara are criminals, and they are more normal than abnormal. Both, however, could benefit from good counseling.

We can also look through these different lenses at the sex scandal in the Catholic Church. We can use the models to speculate why church leaders responded to their pedophilia priests and scandal in the ways they did and do.

Before the public exposure of cover ups, many bishops took a moral approach toward most pedophile priests. They absolved a priest's sins, and the priest perpetrator would promise, with good or bad will, to do penance, make amends, and change their behavior. Moreover, under the seal of confession, the sins and crimes were not disclosed.

From a psychological perspective, some might wonder why such religious, learned, and powerful men responded in ways that enabled serious harm to innocent people. One could argue that there were various reasons, such as immaturity, misguided intentions, ignorance, incompetence, arrogance, clericalism, embarrassment, and fears of scandal and losing power.

Of course, church leaders still take a moral approach. Psychological help is also offered especially to the intended victims. Reporting accusations to legal authorities as well priests being forbidden to publically act as priests until proven innocent are common procedures. Some accused priests feel that are treated as guilty until proven innocent so that their reputation is unjustly damaged.

As we have seen, many victims harbor hurt and anger toward church leaders who think they have resolved the problems with monetary, therapeutic, legal, and educational responses. Some critics contend that there are few self-initiated transparencies, honest accountabilities, and changes especially in seminary formation, system of government, and lay equality.

My model is psychological and spiritual, and not primarily theological, religious, moral, or legal. From this perspective, let us reflect a bit more on what sex abuse means, and then ways to cope and heal.

Chapter Four

What is Sex Abuse?

WHY IS SEXUAL BEHAVIOR so wrong for one person (wife) and not so wrong according to another (husband)? Why is priest pedophilia especially devastating to the individual victims and the general community? Why and how can solitary porn or secret sex victimize others? How can socially acceptable sex be abusive and less than healthy? We respond to these kinds of questions by first looking at what it means to be sexually abused.

We begin with a primary premise: body (sex) and spirit (love) are interrelated; one does not exist without the other. When and where there is sex, there is spirit, albeit often forgotten, repressed, or in some way not integrated. In short, when I try to separate my body from my spirit, I violate both my body and spirit. With this vision in mind, let us reflect on the core motive of abusive sex: lust—and, the core motive of healthy sex: love.

In contrast to a "lust for life" that proclaims a passionate love, we use lust in its negative sense, namely: as our excessive desire to covet and possess someone or something solely for pleasure and power. Instead of respecting human beings as whole (body, mind, and spirit), sex abusers try to reduce their victims to less than they are—spiritless bodies.

Furthermore, sex abusers repress or forget how they are connected to others, especially to those who trust and love them. Sex abusers act as if they are solely individuals whose behavior has no effect on others, as if they are cut off from their loved ones.

An abuser might argue that what he does in private is nobody's business but his own, and as long as loved ones don't know, it won't harm them. Not so. Such reasoning is outdated, naïve, and mistaken, and contrary to basic tenets of both science and spirituality. Because we are interconnected, whatever we do more or less affects others, especially our loved ones.

Moreover, keep in mind that our thinking and behavior highly influences what and who we become. When we invest ourselves in less than healthy sex, our behavior molds our views, feelings, and urges toward intimacy.

For example, pornographic activities will influence a man's intimate relations with his wife. He may expect his wife to be in service of him, or be prone to see her as a body to possess for pleasure rather than an embodied spirit to love. He "has sex" with his wife instead of "being in sexual love" with her.

In contrast to lust, love is at the opposite end of the continuum of connection. Unlike lust, love does not fragment (despiritualize) sex or forget loved ones. When you love, you keep others in mind and heart. Since sex abusers exclude or minimize the spiritual in sex, they forget their loved ones, or they choose to value their abusive experience over the welfare of their loved ones.

Unlike lust, healthy love includes trust and fidelity and honors a person's dignity and integrity. Love does not reduce and use another to a body void of spirit. In love, we see and respond to the whole person—body, mind, and spirit.

In short, when sex abusers forget or repress spiritual realities (love, honor, fidelity, etc.), they are prone to see and use people as objects for self-gratification. Instead of choosing love, they seek lustful self-satisfaction. From this perspective, sex abuse is a violation and betrayal primarily because of its spiritual transgressions.

What is Sex Abuse?

Listen to Stan who frequently enters the reductionist world of lust. "No, I don't brag about looking at internet porn. Although I think a lot of guys do it, I wouldn't talk about it in social gatherings, nor would my wife be happy to hear about it, and I certainly wouldn't recommend it to my children.

"Nevertheless, I get on line for a few hours a week, and at other times I spend three or more hours a day on porn. And when my wife and kids are away, I'm capable of spending eight or more hours a day. True, that's more than a bit much.

"Still, I have to admit that it's a relief to lose myself in the heat of sex. I forget about everything; it's as if my whole world condenses into intense sex. Life comes alive, and nothing is boring or problematic. It's as if I'm immersed in a stimulating yet comfortable fog of pleasure."

Like Stan, sex abusers experience so-called positive effects, such as pleasure, comfort, riskless intimacy, inexhaustible curiosity, and unbridled power. Indeed, if such sexual behavior were painful, few would pursue it. Nevertheless, the negative effects, like the waste of time and energy, diminution of freedom and dignity, narcissistic behavior, lack of love, and harm to others outweigh the supposed positive ones.

Sex abusers, like Stan, can be seen as addicts who obsess about sex and feel compelled to act in ways that do more harm than good. They obsess (persistent and intrusive thoughts) and feel compelled (relentless cravings) to act in untoward, lustful ways in spite of the negative consequences.

The bottom line is that Stan fails to keep his wife and children in mind and heart while in porn. In avoiding conscious contact with his loved ones, he acts as if he his behavior will have no impact on them. To repeat, what we do in private does affect others. Stan's involvement with porn impedes and diminishes his love and unintentionally victimizes those who love him.

Concluding Remarks

Our thesis is that sex abusers look and act with lust and fail to see and act with love. Consequently, sex abusers, whether or not intentional, cause various degrees of harm to self and others. They violate the bond of sex-and-spirit, and therefore demean and diminish you.

You may ask why some people become sex abusers, while others do not? We don't exactly know, but it's safe to say that there is a web of causality, a multiplicity of interconnected forces.

Some possibilities are arrested development, traumatic experiences, inherited predispositions, biochemical imbalance, environmental influences like unhealthy role models and media pressure, bad habits, and the thrill of the chase (pleasure and power).

We do know that sex abusers of whatever type are less than healthy (albeit often normal), but some are worse than others. Pedophiles and rapists are significantly different (criminally, morally, and pathologically) than pornography addicts. Although they are at different places on the spectrum of sex abuse, both are not healthy.

You may wonder if a sex/intimacy abuser can change and become healthy. Know that the addictive part of most sex abusers will do almost anything to maintain their behavior. After all, lust has been an integral part of their lives. Nevertheless, some abusers with help do turn their lives around.

Recovering sex abusers will not only abstain from lustful thoughts and behaviors, but they will also learn healthy attitudes and actions to live good lives. Such changes do not come merely from good intentions, promises, or will power.

Seldom, if ever, is significant and lasting change accomplished alone or quickly, but it demands help from a therapeutic program or competent counseling, or both. Thus, the offender can benefit from programs, such as Sexaholics Anonymous, that offer honest care and understanding, guidelines for healthy living, and compassionate accountability.

The remainder of the book is about how you can cope effectively with a sex abuser of whatever kind and degree, heal from the betrayal, and renew your dignity and integrity. Let us begin with the beginning—when you initially discover that the one you knew or trusted is a sex abuser.

Chapter Five

You Find Out

"I'll never forget the day when I discovered videos and letters of my husband having sexual relationships with elderly women. To say the least, I was numb, dumbfounded, and practically catatonic. I simply stared into space. I wanted to scream, but nothing came out. There was only deafening silence. Then I began to shake with overwhelming fear and anxiety.

"Questions swirled in my mind. My God, who is this man who has been my husband and father of our children for the past twelve years? Have I been married to a depraved gigolo? God, most of the women he had sex with are as old as or older than our parents.

"As I later found out, these women would feed him with food, sex, money, and gifts. They'd serve him and be grateful for his amorous favors. Yet, I don't much blame them. In fact, eventually I came to feel some strange kinship with them, for my husband used and abused them and me.

"I think he took advantage of some very vulnerable women. As I discovered, he had a couple of relationships that lasted a few years. He even maintained one while we were engaged to be married.

"Before I confronted him, I wanted to come out of my fog and grogginess and be more focused and secure. I talked to my brother and a good friend about my situation. They listened with compassion and offered me some helpful advice.

"Although I felt like throwing up on him, I wanted to be rational. Remember, not only was my marriage at stake, but my children's welfare was in jeopardy. Although my husband is a sex pervert, he's a pretty good father, or at least the children think so. Really, I think God was guiding me.

"I first confronted him with the box of generic, sex videos. Well, he was a bit flustered and insulted that I would confront him. He explained that the videos belonged to a co-worker, and he planned to return them. He said that he too was disgusted with how anyone could have sex with so many decrepit women

"Enough of these lies. I gave him a chance to be honest and come clean. So, I showed him the second box, and told him I read the letters and watched the videos of him having sex with his so-called decrepit women. I warned him to avoid giving me the line about a co-worker who just happens to be his identical twin. Now, he was in shock. He was the proverbial deer staring in the headlights.

"The next day he said that he was sorry, and that he didn't want to tell me because he was afraid that I wouldn't understand. He said that he loved me, and that he didn't want to hurt my feelings. He felt guilty and ashamed, and realized that he has a problem. He also apologized for lying, and said that it wasn't easy deceiving me and living two lives. It was a heavy burden. Then he cried.

"I stayed with Vincent for a while. He stopped counseling after a few months, and never took my suggestion to attend S.A. meetings. However, I joined and still participate in S-Anon. He never seemed to understand how deeply his unfaithfulness and deception hurt me, and how he used lonely, trusting, and vulnerable women.

"After considerable sharing and discussing, especially in my S-Anon meetings, I decided to divorce this man. Although I care for him as a human being, I no longer love him as a spouse. Not only do I think it's better for me, but it's better for him as well.

"When I look back, I realize that my head was in the sand, and that our marriage was not as good as I thought. Along with some occasional slips, I keep my serenity and have regained my dignity. Thank God, I've learned and grown a lot. A new life is emerging. I'm emerging."

It's shocking to find that the person you loved and trusted is very different than whom you thought. As we explained in chapter one, our first reaction is often disbelief. You may anxiously rationalize that it couldn't be this bad, or there must be some reasonable explanation. This cannot be!

When you realize that he has deceived and manipulated you, indulged in sex without you, and betrayed you, you'll probably be dazed, frozen, and bewildered. You may want to scream, and yet be speechless. You may want to do something, but feel stuck. You may feel queasy, nauseous, and simply sick. Suddenly your world has drastically changed.

You may want to shake him and make him understand the harm he has done. You want to pound sense into him, to awaken him, to give him some feeling of how much you hurt. With frustration and fury, you wonder if he'll ever understand. He just doesn't get it.

While you're in this initial phase, it's important to accept your reactions, for they help you to manage, or to keep your head above water. Few people stay in this protective place, and you'll eventually come to get your life in better order.

Meanwhile, try to avoid feeling guilty about how you feel, doubting or criticizing your reactions, thinking that you should be doing better, and beating up on yourself. Accept that for the time being, this is the place for you to be.

How others respond to you at this time is also important. Keep in mind that you are very vulnerable, and people can influence you for better and worse. Your sex abuser can especially affect you, often negatively.

For example, he may blame you for being angry and not letting go of the past. Or, he may criticize you for being cold, indifferent, uncooperative, or lacking understanding and affection. By focusing on you, he can confuse and disrupt you and take the focus off himself.

Thus, it's important to share with trustworthy and knowledgeable people, like competent counselors and healthy friends. Be wary of the perpetrator and those in collusion with him.

Because your life has turned upside down and inside out, wait until you settle before making any long-term decisions. Ideally, you want to feel and be right. To be sure, there are exceptions to this guideline, like being put in serious jeopardy. If doable, give yourself time and space to heal so that you can think, choose, and act prudently.

Feeling and Being Dissed

The framework of being "dissed" is another way to understand being victimized. The prefix "dis" aptly points to how you did and perhaps still do feel. Dis expresses negation, reversal, absence, removal, separation, and expulsion; indeed: victimization.

What was once positive is negative. What you thought was present is absent. Where you used to feel at home and secure, you now feel separated, expelled, and alone. The list of how you have been dissed seems unending. Here are some of them; you can add to the list.

Surreal feelings of disbelief may engulf you. You wonder who he is and who you are. Along with such disillusionment, you may feel disjointed and disjunctive, torn apart from whom you trusted and what you thought was true.

You may feel that you are disintegrating—breaking up and breaking down. Disorder, disorganization, dishevelment, distraction, disaccord, disaffiliation, disillusionment, disenchantment, and distaste may permeate you.

You may feel distraught and disabled. What you once rested upon is pulled from under you. Your ground becomes quicksand. To say that you feel discomfort and dismayed is an understatement.

Keep in mind that you are a victim—a person who has been separated from what and whom you held sacred. Whether deliberate or not, the victimizer disparaged and dispensed, dismissed, discounted, discarded, and disdained you.

Understandably, you may feel dislocated and displaced. Indeed, the abuser displaced you with his selfish and lustful behavior. He disregarded, discounted, and disconnected you, and you feel disheartened, disgusted, and disgraced.

You may even feel disembodied and dissociated. You may feel like you're watching a horror movie that you can't end. You may feel that you're outside your body, as if this is not happening to you. You may feel disfigured and disrobed so that you don't quite recognize the person you see in the mirror.

This abyss of dis will eventually dissipate, but its scars and memories will probably linger. They will remind and move you to build a better future.

Believe that your "disses" will challenge you to grow stronger and be better. Your disillusionment will lead to more realistic vision, distortions to clearer thinking, disorder to order, discouragement to confidence, disengagement to enthusiasm, disgust to joy, disgrace to honor, disdain to worth, desolation to consolation, disintegration to integration, disharmony to peace, disfigurement to beauty, disbelief to faith, despair to hope, disheartenment to love.

Are these false promises? Can they come true? Yes, you can realize them. Indeed, your wounds will heal, but you will always have scar tissue to remind you of how far you have come and how strong you are. You will smile with grateful tears.

Compounding Matters

Compounding matters, the sex abuser may impede your efforts to regain your equilibrium. He know the tricks to manipulate, confuse, blame, and disturb you as well as how to minimize his own culpability. He is a veteran of deception.

In contrast to the abuser, you are a novice in coping with such madness. Consequently, it's common to over or under react to his bizarre behavior. To protect yourself, consider some ploys that many addicts (of whatever kind) will use to distract and upset you.

Consider Carol's situation. It's a bit different than our other sex abuse scenarios. Reflect on what you think and feel. What side do you take—hers or her husband's?

"Steve tells me that I'm overreacting. He says that most guys do it, and that it's not a big deal. Even some of my friends concur, and say that's the way men are. Maybe I'm wrong. So, what am I talking about?

"Well, for starters, my husband subscribes to magazines that have pictures of naked women. He also rents and buys pornographic movies, and he wants me to have sex with him while watching them.

"I feel uncomfortable with this sleazy stuff. Although I'm no flaming feminist, these movies are very sexist in that women are invariably seen and used as sex objects, as submissive to dominant men, and are simply demeaning. They're also ageist in that invariably the so-called actors are young and fit the sexist stereotype of being attractive. And besides, the productions are artistically pathetic.

"Most importantly, they have nothing to do with love. Look, I'm open to learning new ways to enjoy sex, and believe me, I love sex. Porn, however, impedes, mocks, and even violates my love making. I simply don't think it's healthy.

"My husband argues that I analyze too much and that my puritanical upbringing has put too many restrictions and guilt trips on me. When I refuse to engage in his adolescent fantasies, he calls me the church lady who thinks she is better than others.

"His comments are insulting. Moreover, he shifts the blame on me, while justifying his own base behavior. Simply stated, I think Steve is wrong and I'm right. Why should I submit myself to something that I think is at best, immature, and at worst, sick, or at least sinful?

"When I ask my husband if he would recommend these media to our teenage and young adult children, he reluctantly says no. Then why would you practice it if you can't recommend it to your children?"

What do you think? Is Carol puritanical, judgmental, narrow-minded, afraid, controlling, old-fashioned, or simply not with it? Is Steve hip, imaginative, fully alive, and right? Or, does Carol hold to healthy values and attitudes? Is she right in arguing that her husband's views and his pornography are less than healthy?

Listen to Steve. "Really, I don't get it, and I don't want to get it. I think Carol is wrong. I think she overacts because of her puritanical upbringing and guilt. She has to learn to let go of that crap and be free. Life is tough enough, why make it tougher? After all, we only live once.

"Let's be real. Porn is a multi-billion dollar industry. Could so many people be wrong? What's the problem? Look, I've tolerated her rigid and closed-minded views. I think that she needs help, not me.

"Why wouldn't I recommend porn to my children? That's easy. It's because they are simply too young to handle such material. When they are of the appropriate age, then they can choose for themselves. Look, if something makes you feel good, then it's good. Right?"

Indeed, behaviors such as pornography, cybersex, and promiscuity are common, acceptable, legal, and lucrative—and, they are less than healthy. As we have indicated, the mistake of many "normal" sex abusers is to use individual need satisfaction and functionality as their sole criteria for health.

Steve is not right because he reduces women to sex objects to use (ego) for his pleasure (body). He seems to be unaware of the love (spirit) dimension of sex.

Although Steve functions well and feels good, he sees and treats himself and others as less than he and they are. He represses or forgets and violates the paramount part of life—healthy intimacy.

Carol is an unintentional victim because her husband violates what she holds most sacred—love. Compounding matters, he fails to accept and respect her views, and tries to impose his own on her. She is a victim—cut off from healthy intimacy.

We contend that Steve is on the spectrum of sex/intimacy abuse. In fact, mass media and society often enable and normalize such sex/intimacy abuse. For example, some T.V. sit-coms would ridicule Carol and favor her husband's ways. We contend that people like Carol are victims of sex abuse

Like Steve, sex abusers often play blame games. If only you wouldn't be so puritanical, moralistic, and judgmental, you would be free to enjoy life. If only you would have been more understanding, less critical, more attractive, sexier, or whatever, he might not have done what he did, so he says. It's not me who is wrong, but you're the problem.

He may persist in analyzing your problems, implying that you and he are equal or have the same culpability. He will fish until he gets a bite; that is, he will try anything to get you to react, to throw you back on yourself, to get you to doubt yourself.

He may focus on your feelings rather than on the issues. Instead of responding to your questions, he accuses you of being angry, unreasonable, and unapproachable. He may criticize you for harping on the subject, for not letting go of the past, and for not forgiving. Before you know it, the spotlight is on you. It is as if you are the perpetrator, and he is the victim.

To that end, he may minimize his issues with inane declarations, such as everyone makes mistakes, nobody's perfect, it's not that bad, or it could be worse. Though containing some truth, such statements serve to minimize the gravity of his behavior as well as circumvent responsibility and accountability.

If these approaches fail—that is, the abuser does not get what he wants—then he may seemingly collapse and cry. Be careful, his apparent weakness and vulnerability often weaken your defenses and appeal to your co-dependent care.

He can seduce you with tears that evoke consolation and compromise. If tears fall short of his goals, he may promise to do and give you anything you want (as long as his addictive self gets what he wants). Before you know it, you may feel sorry for him, and perhaps guilty for upsetting him.

He may promise to never do "it" again. Be careful, for out of fear, most people can change for a short time. If his intent is to avoid getting help and facing the harm he has done to you and himself, he will probably return to his previous behavior.

If blaming, defocusing, crying, and promising are unsuccessful, he'll become frustrated and likely get angry or withdraw. Since he's afraid of losing his sources of comfort—pleasure and power, he'll fight.

He may scare and threaten you. He may scream that you are cold, heartless, and don't understand. He may try to demean you, and forcefully recite a litany of your faults. He may try to corner you into submission. He will try to pull you down to his level.

Since anger evokes anger, it is difficult to avoid being drawn into a battle, which is fought on his grounds. You can become just as angry as he is and lose focus and control. Try to avoid angry arguments, for they seldom do any good, and usually do harm. In the next chapter, we will look at a few other common assumptions and behaviors to avoid.

Chapter Six

What to Avoid

UNDERSTANDABLY, WHEN UNDER EXTREME stress, we can react foolishly, and fall into behaviors that hinder more than help. In our attempts to reduce tension and feel better, we can make things worse. With good intentions, we can try to put out fires with fuel. Let us look at some of these common pitfalls.

The Four Cs

The fours Cs means that you did not cause your trusted or loved one's problem, neither can you cure him, nor can you change him, and you cannot control him.

Theoretically, these statements may be easy to grasp and accept, but experientially it's not so easy. What we know in our head may not translate into behavior. Like many issues, what seems simple may be complex and daunting.

You probably realize that you didn't cause your loved one's addiction. Nevertheless, demons of doubt can undermine what you know. For instance, you may hear whispers in your mind—maybe if I'd have been more attractive or satisfied his needs, he wouldn't have done his shameful deeds. What did I do wrong? Such self-accusations and abasements get you nowhere good.

A common assumption is that if you are the cause, then you can be the cure. The truth is that you didn't cause his problems, and you can't cure him. You simply don't have that kind of power.

Even the founders of the great religions neither could nor did they try to manipulate people. Although they offered better ways to live, they never changed people without their co-operation.

Actually, when we try to control or change someone other than ourselves, matters usually get worse. However, we can help ourselves as well as others who are willing and able to change for the better.

We can learn to act, not react. We can be good role models, giving what we want to receive. We can hope for everything, and expect nothing. We can want and not need someone to change.

Dependent Behaviors

When suffering acute pain, it's not always easy to avoid dependent or pre-addictive behaviors. Thus, you may seek relief or escape to comfort zones that eventually cause more harm than good. Think of how tempting it is to eat, drink, work, play, sleep, and have sex too much to relieve discomfort and feel better.

Drinking, for example, can be tempting because it can be like a solitary affair without the complexity of interpersonal involvement. In a sense, alcohol (or other drugs) is your lover that lessens your pain and gives respite, peace, and the promise of a pleasant buzz.

Mr. Alcohol (or Mr. or Ms. Drug, Food, Work, Sex, Fantasy, Computer, etc.,) is there for you when you need or want him. He is available and reliable with no risk of betrayal. He will comfort you, numb your pain, and help you to forget for a while. Your painful nonsense problems seem to fade and don't matter or hurt as much.

Actually, when you do almost anything too much or too often, you simply don't function as well as when you are clean and sober. Although such self-medicating does have its benefits, it rarely resolves anything, and eventually the negative outweighs the positive.

Furthermore, you jeopardize yourself. You make yourself an easy target particularly for the abuser. For instance, he can focus on you, and question your ability to manage and care for your children. Once again, he can take the focus off himself, and judge you as being the same or worse than he is.

If you struggle with any substance or behavior, get help. Join and participate in a recovery program. You will learn to understand and cope with the nature and dynamics of addictions and co-addictions. With the exception of some time and energy, you have little to lose, and much to gain.

Pitfalls of Thinking and Feeling

A common mistake is to have unrealistic expectations. For example, you might assume that if you are honest and sincere, your abuser will meet you half way. Or you expect your unconditional love will get him to change. When we countenance to unwise expectations, we usually end up feeling frustrated, angry, and miserable.

When we expect bread and get nuts and bolts at the hardware store, we'll be frustrated, perhaps angry, and certainly undernourished. Likewise, when we need and expect the sex abuser to give us what he's unwilling or unable to give, we get psychological nuts and bolts instead of life giving bread.

We can also harbor negative attitudes toward our feelings. For instance, we can get down on ourselves for feeling down, critical for feeling tired, and angry for being angry.

Instead of fighting our feelings, whatever they may be, we can welcome them. We can listen to our anger, anxiety, and self-doubt, and respond to their message. For instance, is our anger due to unrealistic expectations, or is our anger a valid protest against unjust behavior and a means to protect ourselves—or, both?

Besides yourself and the abuser, others may also become critics, judgers, and blamers. They may tell you that you are too angry, and unknowingly reinforce your negative thinking. Some of the abuser's family and friends may accuse you of being a cause of their loved one's problems. Avoid pleading guilty to such false charges.

Instead, share your thoughts and feelings with wise, trustworthy, and concerned people. Listen to what they say, reflect on their advice, and keep contact with them. Avoid isolating or trying to change on your own. Self-sufficiency that excludes others is a mistake. Don't be alone on your journey of recovery.

Sometimes, you may have to fake it in order to make it. This doesn't mean that you are phony, but rather that you act your way into thinking and feeling better. You may have to follow a script is that you put in your mind and post on your refrigerator. You may have to do the right thing in order to feel and be right. Remember, what you think and do is what you become.

The bottom line is to accept and honor how you think and feel. Without judgment, believe that you can listen to what your feelings are telling you. To that end, seek competent people, like wise friends, counselors, ministers, and veteran S-Anon members to help you.

It may also be helpful to keep a personal journal where you periodically record and reflect on your feelings and thoughts. You may also want to read books on co-dependency that question your mistaken beliefs and offer alternatives to better coping.

In time, different ways of thinking, feeling, and behaving will feel natural and right. Like any worthwhile change, it takes time and work, but it does happen, and it will get easier and better.

Chapter Seven

Codependency

ARGUABLY, CO-DEPENDENCY IS THE most common impediment to coping effectively with problematic people. It may be the most well intentioned attempt to improve matters that results in making matters worse. It is a classic example of unintended consequences.

If you are or have been involved with a sex abuser, you are likely to be co-dependent, or a "co-addict." Indeed, such a statement may irritate or even infuriate you, because he is the problem, not you. Yes, he (or she) is the problem, but with good intentions, you probably enabled him.

Being co-dependent may sound like a dire admission, but actually it's positive because your co-dependency is something you can change. You can change the way you interact with and respond to the abuser, and thus improve your situation. Let's look at what co-dependency means, and what you can do about it.

The prefix of co-dependent, "co," literally means that you are or have been involved "with" a person who is too dependent on sex (or any process or substance). A "co-sexaholic" person is "tied up with" a person who has serious problems with sex and intimacy.

It means that you have unwittingly trusted and cared for, perhaps needed, and may have enabled a sex abuser.

You may have been the sex abuser's dance partner, dancing to his music and following his lead. Once again, the good news is that you can play different music, change your steps, and dance with the angels.

When we are co-dependent, we care, seemingly unconditionally, but often to our own detriment. Our flaw is that we trust, look up to, and get too much of our well-being from the sexaholic. Thus, we are prone to do almost anything for our sex abuser in order to satisfy our need to feel good. Our common mistake is that our well-being lies too much with another and not enough within our self.

Simply stated, when the abuser is happy and up, you are happy and up. When he is unhappy or down, you are unhappy or down. Consequently, you are prone to do almost anything to get him to be content or satisfied, because then you feel better. Your mistake is that you need the abuser to change for you to feel well.

For instance, when you didn't know that your loved one was a sex abuser, you probably engaged in co-dependent behavior. You gave him whatever he wanted, minimized his negative behavior, gave more credence to his thinking than yours, and trusted him too much. With love and trust, you enabled what and who hurt you.

You may have unknowingly given your abuser too much power and control. You may have reluctantly acquiesced to his style of living so that you acted in ways that were against your values, while repressing uneasy feelings about his behavior.

When you discover that your loved one is quite different than you thought, your co-dependency may still continue but in a different form. Now, you need him to be contrite, reasonable, honest, and so forth, placing too much of your welfare in his hands, and thereby empowering him. In short, you depend too much on a dependent person, or you are "co-dependent."

If we need the other to change to feel better, we'll try to do almost anything to get our abuser to be or do what we need. We might try to please him, to give him what he wants. We might try to follow his suggestion to forgive, forget, and get on with it.

Another futile tactic to get him to wise up is to be passive aggressive. For instance, you give him the "ice water" treatment, that is, you act distant and cold, as if you don't care. You carry a chip on your shoulder and bear a negative attitude. You may deny being angry, and refuse to talk about it.

Or you may be blatantly angry and engage in heated arguments. You call him names, degrade and demean him, and provoke and try to intimidate him. You threaten to expose him, give him ultimatums, try to evoke guilt, and overall shame him. Wanting him to hurt as much as you hurt, you try to give him a taste of his own medicine. Maybe then, he will see the light, and change.

Instead of moving against or toward the sexaholic, you may move away from him. You try to disappear and make yourself unavailable. You think that if he really cares about you, he'll miss you. Maybe your absence will make him understand and truly love you.

In all of these scenarios, you are trying to do the impossible—to change the abuser for the better. Realize that when you need him to change, you will feel pressured to manipulate him. After all, you feel that your well-being is at stake.

As we have indicated and will continue to explain, your well-being must come primarily from trustworthy persons within and around you. Then, you will feel basically secure, strong, and serene regardless of what the he does.

Pause, look and listen, and reflect. If you need the sexaholic to understand or "get it," need him to appreciate your pain, know the harm he has done, be truly sorry, and make amends in order for you to feel better, you're in trouble.

If you need him to stop criticizing, blaming, and analyzing you, you're in trouble. If you need him to disappear, get out of your life, or die, you're in trouble. If you need the sexaholic to change for you to be free, you're in trouble.

To "want" your abuser to change is fine. Indeed, life would probably be better for you, and for him as well. However, to "need" him to be healthy for you to be okay is co-dependent and not the better way.

Why Are We Co-Dependent?

There are many possible reasons why we may be co-dependent. The prevalent one is that we care. When you love someone, you desire what is best for that person. You want to help him be and feel better, to be happy. You are willing to do almost anything to increase the welfare of the one you love. Thus, it's easy to slip into co-dependency.

A common mistake is to follow a one-sided conception of love. When we are co-dependent, we are prone to construe love as doing what is best for the other, while forgetting ourselves. You may be willing to say and do almost anything to be loved. In short, someone, like an abuser of intimacy, can take advantage of our vulnerability, trust, and love.

A healthier view of love is choosing to do what is best for "us"—both you and me. Instead of putting others before ourselves, we have to learn to take just as good care of ourselves. In a sense, we have to reverse the golden rule. We also have to do unto ourselves as we do unto others.

Another possible reason is that we may come from a co-dependent background. For instance, you may have learned to pattern your behavior after a good person whom you admired, but who didn't have a healthy sense of boundaries. You may have patterned your behavior after a co-dependent parent who took care of a problematic person, like an alcoholic or abusive spouse.

Authority figures, like teachers, pastors, and parents, may have taught you that being a good person is to be responsible for the welfare of others. We may have learned that good people sacrifice themselves to make others happy. In doing so, we learned to believe that we can and should do the impossible, "make" people happy. With good intentions, we believed an illusion—that we have more power then we really have.

Some of us seem to have a deep call to serve others that for some reason gets out of bounds. Again, we put others before ourselves. To be sure, we should love and make sacrifices for others, but not to the detriment of our health. To reaffirm, our challenge is to love both self and others.

An unfortunate and frequent reason we become co-dependent is the result of deficiencies in our early development. What we deserved, we did not get, namely: our basic needs were not sufficiently satisfied. Clearly, this is not our fault, but it does put us at a disadvantage.

Like a child, we are apt to look outside ourselves for our trust, security, and esteem. Some of us wear a sign that reads: "I need love and I'm willing to do almost anything to get it." Discard signs that advertise your needs. The sex offender can read them from a mile away.

Enabling

"Indeed, this is and has been embarrassing, for I should have known better. Look, I'm a counselor who deals with troubled families as well as some drug addicts. However, in my defense, I haven't dealt with any sex addicts, at least ones like my husband. Nevertheless, it's been humbling and humiliating.

"I've heard and read a little bit about cybersex, but I never thought it would happen in my own house. I never dared to admit that the man I've slept with for the past 23 years has been in porn most of his life, and the last 10 years in internet sex. I bow to the power of denial and rationalization.

"I have to admit that I sensed that something was amiss in our marriage. It sort of got dry and sterile, lacking juice and enthusiasm. No longer were we passionate with each other, nor did we simply have fun together or enjoy each other. In retrospect, I can see that I buried my head in the sand by becoming a workaholic.

"I really couldn't bear to look at what was happening to our lives. With civility, we were growing apart, while failing to practice what I advised other couples to do. Admittedly, it's easier to look at others than at yourself. I simply did not walk my talk.

"One day I happened to stumble on to a bill that seemed to be for computer sex. When I asked him about it, he said that most men do it and that it was no big deal. Indeed, I didn't want it to be a big deal, so I accepted his explanation.

"Nevertheless, the bill wouldn't leave my mind. So a few weeks later, I checked his laptop, and found an enormous amount of pornographic websites. After looking at a few of them, I felt sick.

"Well, after a few months of his deception and my anxiety, a friend confronted me with the reality that I was facilitating the behavior that was driving me nuts. Theoretically, I knew about enabling, but I never truly admitted that I was an expert enabler. My friend strongly and lovingly encouraged me to join S-Anon.

"Thank God for S-Anon. I'm not overstating the matter when I say that the fellowship and the program saved my sanity. I learned to stop enabling, to set appropriate boundaries, and to take good care of myself.

"Ironically, in this way I actually helped my husband. Without my enabling, he was is more likely to face himself and think about changing his life. Regardless of what he does, I will continue to foster and enjoy my own well-being."

Give this woman credit. She is a professional counselor who humbly admitted her faults and sought and accepted help from non-professionals. She learned to change her co-dependent attitudes and behaviors. Along with helping others, she learned to help herself.

Remember that a co-dependent/co-sexaholic will do practically anything to change or fix the sexaholic in order to feel good. Unwittingly, she places her happiness in the hands and control of a troubled person. Indeed, enabling is a common cause of making matters worse—and, that's something you can change.

If the more you do, the worse things get, it's likely that you are an enabler. It's as if you are trying to extinguish a fire with gasoline that you mistakenly think is water. You expect the fire to diminish, but instead it increases. You are baffled, frustrated, and at wits end.

Codependency

Listen, you can come to realize the subtle ways in which you enabled your sexaholic, and change the way you respond. Like the counselor, you may have let your marriage slip into sterile civility. You might have minimized or rationalized questionable behavior.

With trust and good will, you may have given him too much power and control over financial affairs. Perhaps he handled the bills, buying, and savings without your input, enabling him to do almost anything with the money. For instance, when you look in retrospect, most purchases and leisure activities were centered on his interests.

Overall, you treated him better than you treated yourself. With periodic exceptions, you found yourself doing things his way, deferring to him, and going along to get along. Compounding matters, you may have been too grateful for the ordinary, like helping out with household chores and spending time with the children.

To reaffirm, in spite of your co-dependency, the sex abuser's betrayal, lies, manipulation, exploitation, and deception victimized you. Although you unintentionally enabled, you did not cause the abuse. You are a victim, not a perpetrator.

However, since your enabling indirectly facilitated, not caused, his behavior, you can stop such negative enabling and learn, in a sense, how to enable positive behavior. Actually, the remainder of the book is about such "positive enabling."

Chapter Eight

The Spiritual Power of Recovery

WE CAN SAY WITH certitude that how we construe and practice spirituality, or not, highly influences how we take care of ourselves and interact with others. Thus, it behooves us to reflect on what is or isn't spirituality, and what difference it may or may not make.

My contention is that when we draw on reliable and valid spiritual resources, we think, choose, and act better. Spirituality is not a panacea, but without it, we weaken ourselves and put ourselves at a disadvantage. With spirituality, we are and do better.

With this in mind, I offer a succinct account of the nature and dynamics of spirituality. My hope is that it will challenge you to reflect on and perhaps improve your own view of spirituality. In the next chapter, I will show how a spiritual approach can empower us to manage sex abusers as well as engender healing, freedom, and serenity. So, what is this spiritual resource?

Simply stated, I see spirituality as living a virtuous life that includes a reality greater than and part of ourselves. In short, virtuous living is the art of practicing good habits (such as compassion, kindness, mercy, prudence, fortitude, gratitude, and faith, hope, and love) that empower us to seek and achieve unity and peace within ourselves and with others.

Part of being a spiritual person is to connect with a reality that is part of and greater than our self. There are many names for this spiritual reality, such as Higher Power, Universal Self, Tau, Being, Nothingness, Uncreated Energy, Truth, Beauty, and Love. Call this reality whatever or whoever you want. I call this reality: God, or uncreated/co-creating Love.

This Higher Power, or God, is both imminent (part of us) and transcendent (greater than us). If we seriously believe that God resides within, beyond, and in the midst of us, then we can connect and draw from this power of Love for on-going recovery and health.

More important than this pithy, lay theology are its clinical consequences. We will see throughout the remainder of the book that when we connect with a divine reality, we broaden our vision, feel safer and consoled, and are stronger and freer to heal and manage successfully.

It behooves us to foster a constant and conscious contact with a Reality that is greater than and part of our individual (ego) self. It follows that when we forget or refuse to avail ourselves to this Being, we actually weaken ourselves, and when we bond with this power of inexhaustible Love, we are liberated and empowered.

To achieve this spiritual power, it is usually necessary to admit that we are power-less. We come to accept that we have less power than we might assume or want to have, like when we think we can make the sex abuser understand or change. We come to realize that we are not the highest power, and yet, we are part of this Greater Power.

The wonderful paradox is that when we accept our power-lessness and surrender to our Greater Power, we are empowered. Indeed, in weakness, we find our strength. Hopefully, the sex offender will also come to this breakdown (of ego) that leads to a breakthrough (spirit) to a better life.

We will show how we can learn to attach to our spiritual resources, so that we can detach from the sex/intimacy abuser, protect and console ourselves, and love and manage effectively. Spirituality, not psychology alone, becomes our power base to heal our wounds and to cope effectively.

Like any activity, to maintain and improve our spiritual life, we must practice it. As the saying goes, we must use it or lose it. Fortunately, we have access to many Western and Eastern spiritual traditions that offer time-tested ways to practice the spiritual life. Most include prayer, meditation, contemplation, communal worship, support groups, spiritual direction, service to self and others, and overall ways to help ourselves and others live a better life.

Finally, it helps a doubting Thomas like me to know that empirical research supports our psycho-spiritual approach at least insofar as people who practice a positive spirituality (and religion) tend to live longer and healthier lives. Rather than being an illusion, a God or Love centered spirituality can be an effective and smart way to maintain, nourish, and facilitate our spiritual and mental health.

Hopefully, these succinct views will help and challenge you to explore and reflect on how you construe spirituality, religion, and God—and, what difference it makes in your life. To that end, I offer you ways to practice the spiritual life, the ways of HABITS.

Chapter Nine

HABITS

"HABITS" IS AN ACRONYM that refers to a method of practicing spirituality that is particularly relevant to stressful situations, such as being a victim of sex/intimacy abuse. Each letter points to part of a process that builds good habits or virtues to manage and heal.

HABITS stands for H: halt and hover; A: admit and accept; B: breathe and be; I: intend and insert; T: think and try; and S: strength and serenity. Let us begin with "H"—halt and hover.

Halt and Hover

As we have seen, when you first discover that the person you loved or trusted is a sex offender, you feel radically dissed and spiritually wounded. For better and/or worse, you sense that your life will never be the same. We have already touched on what to avoid. Now what can you do?

When you feel hurt, confused, scared, angry, or however upset, your first challenge is to do practically nothing. Instead of reacting to what the abuser says or does, you halt and hover.

Before doing or saying anything, slow down and become aware of what your perceiving, thinking, and feeling. Pause and hover over what's happening. As difficult and unfair as it may feel, try to relax as much as you can. Instead of getting uptight, let be. When you literally or metaphorically notice your clenched fist, try to open and relax it. Paradoxically, doing nothing is the first step in doing something.

Actually, you take control of yourself. You curb impulses to react, to get emotionally labile, to argue, to acquiesce, to plead and please, to be passive aggressive, to be mean, to try to change the abuser. You protect yourself, and you halt futile reactions. You slow down and wait. Indeed, this is easier said than done.

One way of just being present without fixing things is to pause and pray. When we feel pressured, it's a signal to stand still and connect with your greater (than just your ego) power, or with the God of your understanding.

You might say a brief prayer. For example, you might repeat internally the serenity prayer, or silently chant a saying or mantra, like "Om," "Namaste," "God, help me." "Let go and let God," or any words or practice that settle and center you.

If you don't pray, you can pause, step back, and gain perspective. You can remind yourself to relax and settle as well as to affirm and comfort yourself. You can connect with the power within you rather than focusing on the abuser.

If he pressures you to speak or make a decision, buy time to pause, pray, and reflect on the issues and perhaps consult with someone. You might say something like I'll get back to you later. The point is not to let him force you to react according to his wants and needs. You take control.

Admit and Accept

The next step on our journey of empowerment is to admit and accept what is happening. Admit means to own up to what we feel and think: to name, claim, and accept our feelings rather than fighting or feeling guilty about them.

HABITS

For example, admit that you are powerless (not helpless) over the abuser. You remind yourself that you can't fix or change him, or make him understand, be reasonable, or anything else. To repeat, the wonderful paradox is that when you admit that you have less power than you think or would like to have, you are already being liberated and empowered.

Acceptance means that we are aware of what is happening and that we don't "need" the offender to change, even though we prefer changes. Rather than fighting or trying to change what you cannot change, you can deflect what is hurled at you. You can push aside negative energy, like insults, lies, and manipulations, so that it doesn't distort your perception of what is happening.

Rather than getting trapped in an argument, you can accept (neither condone nor condemn) his lack of understanding and reasonableness, and deflect his unfair or inadequate responses. Instead of engaging his comments, you push them aside, and for the time being give them little or no consideration.

So far, we are saying that you can pause, pray, admit, accept, and deflect what is happening. This means that instead of moving outward, you first move inward and take care of yourself. You don't look to the abuser for what you want or need, but you rely on yourself, God, and trustworthy others. Instead of directly engaging the abuser, you protect and empower yourself.

Breathe and Be

Our next step is to breathe and be—and, this is not as simple and lame as it may sound. To the contrary, good breathing settles, centers, and empowers you. However, when dishonesty and insults are thrown at you, it is difficult to avoid holding your breath, breathing quickly, or gulping air.

Instead, learn to breathe rhythmically and smoothly from your diaphragm. (For example, Yoga, Tai Chi, and various forms of meditation teach proper breathing.) Before and after difficult times, take time out to settle, center, and calmly breathe. Such preparatory and retroactive breathing is helpful.

It is even more important to breathe well when or during taxing times. Too often and understandably, we forget to breathe properly when under pressure, threatened, or hurt –or, when we need healthy breathing the most. Instead, breathe when you are stressed, or use your stress as a signal to de-stress.

For example, when you begin to get uptight, start to obsess, or get scared, be mindful of how you are breathing, and settle yourself with proper breathing. To reiterate, don't hold your breath or hyperventilate; instead, breathe rhythmically from your diaphragm. This is something you can do regardless of what the abuser says or does. You'll be surprised how healthy breathing can help you.

As trite as it may sound, you inhale oxygen to energize and nourish, and exhale carbon dioxide to cleanse yourself. You humbly and gratefully take in positive energy and let go of negative energy. You calmly focus and keep your balance.

Psychologically, you can think of inhaling positive thoughts and exhaling false beliefs. When you halt and hover, and admit and accept what is happening outside and inside you, you can breathe to cleanse and energize your body and mind.

From a spiritual perspective, you can breathe from and in your Holy Spirit. (Spirit is derived from the Latin, *spiritus* to breath and *spirare* to breathe.) You take in or connect with your God who abides within you. You can affirm that you are a *theotokos* (the Greek word for God bearer).

Or you might prefer that you inhale the energy of nature, chi, universal self, humankind, or your higher power. However you understand it, while breathing, you take in what helps you and expel what harms you.

In sum, it is wise to learn to breathe well, to inhale the positive and exhale the negative—physically, psychologically, and spiritually. When we breathe well, we are more likely to be well.

Intend and Insert

When you begin to feel more relaxed, balanced, and grounded, you can choose to insert yourself in the reality that is part of and

HABITS

greater than you. Remember that your paramount source of power abides within you, and no one can take that from you.

This greater and imminent power is love for and from God, self, and others. We contend that a community of love lives in us, and it behooves us to insert ourselves in and draw upon it.

Imagine being surrounded by God and people whom you trust and who love you. Image this inner community protecting, consoling, and guiding you. Imagine asking them for advice and favors. Imagine having fun and relaxing with them. They will respond.

Indeed, it is also wise to connect with trustworthy people outside your skin, like family, friends, clergy, counselors, and support groups. And when such people are unavailable, you can draw on your inner community of love.

This notion of inner bonding in and with love may seem abstract, unavailable, or unattainable. Actually, it can be quite concrete and doable.

Think of a person whom you love dearly and who dies. Indeed, your loved one is sorely missed, yet that loving person lives on within you. Paradoxically, even her or his absence is a form of presence that dwells within you as well as guides and comforts you. You can connect with your loved ones so that they still make a difference in your life. Their thoughts, good and difficult times, support and advice, and especially their love live within you. In short, significant people, alive and dead, influence why and how you live. Re-member them.

In this way, special people, whom you have trusted, honored, and loved, living and dead, are part of you. They are present within you to listen to, talk with, and love. With God and self, they are your interior power base, your inner community of love.

Clearly, people you love and trust and who love and trust you become an integral and influential part of you. Unfortunately, this is why your abuser has ripped you apart. You trusted and perhaps loved this man, and he betrayed you. Loved ones, usually not strangers, devastate us.

When you catch yourself in a toxic dance with your sex abuser, you can pause, breathe, pray, and connect with those loving persons who dwell within you. Instead of dancing with the sexaholic, you dance with them. Their music is soothing; their touch is safe; their steps are liberating; their rhythm is enjoyable; their dance is life-giving.

Instead of being co-dependent, you depend on your higher power of Love. Instead of trying to get from the sexaholic what he is unwilling or unable to give, you ask for and receive help from your community of love.

When you are scared, frustrated, or hurt, you can enter your safe and sacred place where you are protected, empowered, and healed. You can halt, accept, breathe, and connect with your energies of love. Instead of depending on the abuser, you accept and let go of him, and let love from God and others empower, guide, and console you.

Think and Try

Anchored in the security and strength of your community of love, take your time to think of what you want to do. Don't let an abuser, or anyone, pressure you to make a decision immediately, or when you're not ready. When you need or want time to consult and think, take it.

Especially when we feel pressured, we can avoid reacting, exploding, or imploding. Instead, we can pause, breathe, pray, and bond within. Instead of becoming overly emotional, we can attach within, detach from the negative, and think. Instead of getting upset and confused with ambivalent and ambiguous emotions, we can attach to our higher power of Love—and, settle and discern.

Before making an important decision, consult with others inside and outside yourself. Share with a few wise people whom you trust and respect. If you partake in a support group, you can ask the members what they did or might do in a similar situation. Moreover, you can ask significant persons, including God, for advice.

For instance, imagine talking to your Jewish, Christian, or Muslim God. Or you might consult Buddhist, Hindu, Taoist, Confucian, Native American, etc. teachings and practices. Whatever your conception of God, or your religious or philosophical tradition, you can listen to its wisdom. You don't have to think, decide, and act alone.

We can see that external action is usually not the first, thing we do. Instead of reacting immediately, we consult, process, and decide when and how we want to respond. And sometimes, the best action is no action.

We can buy time from a few seconds or minutes to hours, days, months, years, or forever. Seldom are matters so important and urgent that we have little or no time to consult and think of what we should or want to do.

Sometimes we have to experiment. We can't be certain about how something will really work until we try it and see the results. If your experiment doesn't work very well, then you can try something else. Remember, you can change your mind.

Strength and Serenity

When we practice HABITS, we come to realize that our ego (reason and "I") and spirit (faith and "we") work together to develop virtues. Indeed, there are many virtues that we can learn, and as we have seen, the paramount one is love.

In fact, we can argue that all our virtues involve and manifest love, and its source and destiny—uncreated/co-creating Love, or God. Serenity and strength (fortitude) are two of the virtues that enable us to think, decide, feel, act, and be better,

Bonding with Love, we become more balanced and at home with ourselves and others. We feel and function better because our serenity and strength do not depend on the abuser, but comes from within and around us. In fact, serenity is a good barometer of how well we are being and doing.

When we lose our serenity, we're weaker, more vulnerable, and probably losing control. It often means that we need someone to change to feel at peace. When this happens, pause and practice your good habits to regain your serenity and strength.

Inserting yourself in your community of love, you are less likely to feel anxious, insecure, vulnerable, weak, vindictive, ashamed, trapped, hopeless, alone. Instead, you come to feel more peace, security, safety, strength, patience, worthiness, freedom, and love.

In this and the preceding chapter, we have proposed that spirituality or a Love centered life is the power base of coping and being better. To concretize the spiritual, we offered a way, HABITS, of practicing the spiritual life in regards to your abuser and life in general.

Next, we will focus on psychological (ego) strategies to cope with our stressful situations. We will see that our management skills are also important to learn, and that it benefits us to draw on both spiritual and psychological resources.

Chapter Ten

Boundaries

Your challenge is to learn to be relatively free and serene regardless of how the intimacy abuser thinks, acts, and feels. To that end, it is important to learn how to practice healthy boundaries. Let us begin with an understanding of why and how boundaries are important.

It's important for us to act within boundaries because they set standards for appropriate conduct. In play, work, interpersonal relationships, or whatever activity, if we don't set, respect, and act within boundaries, we suffer harmful and unnecessary consequences. Indeed, the sex/intimacy abuser acts out of bounds and causes serious problems for you and others.

Boundaries establish how far and in what way you want another to go. When someone crosses your line, he transgresses and violates you. Boundaries not only protect what you have but also who you are.

The first step in setting boundaries is stepping back, or start to practice your spiritual habits. You pause, breathe, accept and deflect what's happening, breathe, and connect with you inner community of love. Securing yourself in this safe and strong place will enable you to set and keep appropriate boundaries.

For instance, you tell the abuser what he is allowed or not allowed to do in regards to you and your loved ones. You tell him what you're willing and unwilling to tolerate and do. Boundaries let the abuser and others know where you stand, and what they can and cannot say and do to and with you.

You can refuse to serve as the abuser's target for shooting insults, lies, and blame. You can connect with your Higher Power, deflect his demeaning remarks, and firmly tell him to stop. If he persists, you can leave the room. You, not him, establish your boundaries. You need not "take" offenses.

You can also set boundaries on what you own. Take control of your possessions and your money, especially if he has spent money on sex. Don't let him determine what you do with what you own.

Protect your personal space. You decide how close he can get to you. You decide where you sleep with or without him. You decide if he can touch you, and if you want to touch him. (Don't be lured into the delusion that sex will resolve matters.) You set the boundaries.

You firmly tell the abuser when he transgresses your boundaries. Don't argue the point, or try to make him understand. Don't need him to respect your boundaries; you respect them. You stop tolerating the intolerable.

However, instead of practicing good habits, we can slip into bad ones. We have seen that when we suffer severe stress, we may be prone to drink, eat, sleep, work, or play too much or too little. Particularly when we are alone, it may be very difficult to set boundaries on our own behavior.

When you fail to maintain your boundaries (as we all do at times), don't catastrophize, beat yourself, or sell yourself short. Connect with trustworthy persons inside and outside yourself, and re-establish your boundaries.

We have also seen that co-dependency and its enmeshment are often the basis of having less than healthy boundaries. When you are tied up with an intimacy abuser, you hardly know the line or space between you and him.

Once again, you are riding on the co-dependent roller coaster. When he is up, you are up, and when he comes down, you travel with him. One of the problems is that the sexaholic controls the ride, and you are taken for a ride. However, you can stop and get off, and find rides that are going somewhere good.

Chapter Eleven

Detachment

A CRUCIAL PRINCIPLE IS that when we attach internally, we are empowered to detach externally. Like setting healthy boundaries, we first connect internally, and then behave externally with detachment. In short, our exterior success depends on our interior status. Listen to Ruth.

"Wow, life is, or I am, very different. No longer do I take my husband's criticism, blame, shame, and guilt. No longer do I get into arguments, or let him hurt me as much as he did. No longer do I swallow my own poison of obsessive thinking, resentment, and hate.

"So, what happened to change me from a naïve co-dependent to a free woman? How did I learn that my welfare no longer depended on my sexaholic husband? How did I get to the place where I can accept with serenity, though detest, what he did and may do again?

"Simply put, I came to admit that I am powerless over my husband, that I cannot change, control, or cure him. And I came to rely on a God and trustworthy people, a Higher Power, who helped me to accept who and what I cannot change.

Detachment

"Indeed, when I turn my life and will to my God, I feel stronger and more secure. Sure, I can still be hurt, but much less than when I needed him to change. In other words, when I attach to my reliable love sources, I can detach from my husband and no longer absorb his crazy-making games. Like in the martial arts, I've learned to deflect his negative energy, and rarely kick back."

This woman contends that her spiritual attachment enables her to detach from her own co-dependencies, manage her husband's ploys, and hurt much less. For her, detachment has been crucial in gaining and maintaining her sanity. So, what is detachment?

When we detach, we separate ourselves from unhealthy attachments, like the need to change someone, boundary enmeshment, or resentment. We detach when our well-being is too attached (tied, stuck) to anyone, especially to an abuser.

Healthy detachment is a way of caring, especially for our self. We have seen that practicing HABITS helps us to maintain our well-being regardless of what the abuser does. Consequently, when he is down, restless, or needy, you can be relatively up, serene, and secure.

We can employ detachment in many ways. For instance, you can detach from your need to have him satisfy your needs. Now you look for peace within yourself rather than from him. In a sense, you need nothing personal from the abuser to maintain your serenity. If he is decent, accept it as a benefit but not a necessity.

You can detach from unrealistic expectations, like your honesty will make him honest, or that your love will change him. You detach from such unrealistic needs, expectations, and assumptions. You flush them where they won't harm you.

Being "un-enmeshed," you avoid absorbing or taking him into you. You set boundaries that prevent him from invading your emotional, mental, and spiritual space. You do not let yourself be lured into his world, or try to lure him out of his world. You let him be.

To reaffirm, our spiritual bonding enables us to detach and focus on the issues at hand. Rather than letting the sexaholic confuse, blame, or trap you, you deflect his ploys. Instead of being drawn into an argument, you push aside his manipulative barbs. Keeping your stand, you refuse to get sucked into his world. Like Ruth, you become a warrior who seldom if ever throws a punch.

Sometimes you may have to detach physically. For instance, if the abuser harasses you, it behooves you to leave the situation. You can excuse yourself and go to a room where you can recollect and center yourself, or get your mind on something else.

You may have to leave the house to get safe and quiet space. In extreme situations, you may have to get him out of the house. You may have to call the police, and get a protection from abuse order. Whatever the case, consult with compassionate and savvy people to help you to think and decide clearly.

It may seem unfair that all of the work is on you, since you didn't cause the problems. This is true, but any other way makes things worse. Remind yourself that when you attach inwardly and detach outwardly, you are in control of your life. Instead of enabling and empowering the abuser, you enable and empower yourself.

Chapter Twelve

Psychological Strategies

SO FAR, WE HAVE discussed how to avoid false beliefs, co-dependency, and unhealthy boundaries, and how to replace them with better behavior. We also proposed a spiritual model as the power base to practice detachment and to maintain healthy boundaries. In light of this psycho-spiritual perspective, consider how the following coping strategies can also help you manage effectively.

Suppression

Simply stated, when we suppress, we say "yes" to our feelings and thoughts, and say "no" to their expression. We freely check them and put them aside. We put them on a shelf, and later decide what to do with them—whether or not and how to express them.

For example, when the abuser hurts you, you can connect with your sources of love and consolation, and suppress your feelings. Then you can choose to tell or not tell him how you think and feel at the moment, later, or never.

A caveat: Sometimes we mistakenly think that we must be "transparent," and share all of what we think and feel. Be careful because such openness can empower the abuser to manipulate you. Blatant expression without any suppression may be well intended, but usually foolish and dangerous.

Or we may think that if we suppress or hold back, we're being dishonest. We're not being dishonest or fabricating, but simply waiting for a better time to share, which may or may not happen. Prudence is important.

Another misconception is to confuse (positive) suppression with (negative) repression. When we suppress, we name and claim, suspend or bracket, and choose an appropriate time and place to express our self. When we repress, we are unaware of our feelings, and therefore lack the freedom to express, deflect, or suppress them.

Understandably, it may be difficult to suppress and avoid reacting when an abuser is pushing your buttons. Although tempting, unbridled expression of feelings seldom resolves anything, and often empowers the abuser.

Say, for instance, that the sex offender refuses to work a program of recovery and minimizes his problems. Indeed, you may get frustrated, scared, and angry. Instead of reacting with angry criticism, you can step back, engage your HABITS, suppress your feelings, and thereby think and manage.

Yes, initially such suppression is easier said than done, but it's not as difficult and complicated as it may initially sound. Like any good (or bad) habit, it comes to be second nature with practice—and, practice.

Sublimation

Sublimation literally means to raise or elevate feelings. When we sublimate, we redirect energy from one activity and invest it in another that is usually judged to be more acceptable, "higher," or better.

For example, when the abuser pushes your buttons, instead of expressing your fury, you can regain your balance with inner bonding, suppress your angry, and later sublimate it by investing the energy in a safe, acceptable, and often productive behavior.

You may engage in some form of physical or intellectual activity to work off your feelings. If you have the time, you can also sublimate with volunteer and charitable activities. You avoid repression or building up a slush fund of pain and anger; rather, you suppress and sublimate.

This woman sublimated in the following ways. "It wasn't easy, but I trained myself to step back when he pushed my buttons. I'd say little or nothing, and I'd put my feelings on the shelf for a while.

"Sooner than later, I'd take out my frustration and anger by cleaning the house and making meals, or I'd tune out with television, or simply pray. With the help of friends and my God, I'd get him out of my system."

When you sublimate, instead of turning your frustration and anger against the abuser, you get your mind off the irritation and invest your energy in productive activities. As the lady said, you get it and him out of your system, not deeper in it.

Anticipation

Anticipation is another helpful coping mechanism. When we anticipate, we foresee what's likely to occur, and we plan to act in ways that prevent or ameliorate negative consequences. It's "as if" we can predict what the abuser will likely do.

Consider this woman's use of anticipation. "When I needed my husband to watch the kids or help me in whatever way, he'd often make excuses that he was too busy or tired. Before I learned, his lame excuses would infuriate me.

"I learned that I simply couldn't depend on him; so I always had alternative plans. When he responded inappropriately, I didn't go into a tail spin, for I always had other plans. I'd pause, breathe, and pray, and employ one of my plans.

"Is this the way I wish it should be? No. Is it fair? No. But, it's a lot better than wasting time and energy being bent out of shape.

For the most part, I stay in control, keep my serenity, and get the job done."

Indeed, you can't predict the future perfectly, but you can do better than chance. Like this woman, you can learn from past experiences what your offender often says and does. Instead of being caught off guard and reacting inappropriately, you're ready to respond appropriately, or like the woman, you can have alternative plans.

Another example is that you learn from repeated experiences that when you bring up certain issues, he'll avoid facing, sharing, and talking about them. Knowing this, you can prepare to maintain your composure and manage your frustration.

Anticipation is not only helpful in dealing with an abuser, but also with oneself. For instance, one of the many acronyms of twelve step programs is HALT. When we are Hungry, Angry, Lonely, or Tired, we are more vulnerable to reacting humanly but foolishly.

We know from past experiences that when we're hungry, we may be irritable. When angry, we may be more likely to react. When lonely, we may need to please. When tired, we may be more vulnerable, volatile, or simply give in to whatever. HALT is a good example and practice of anticipation,

Thus, you can anticipate your reactions, and take measures to protect and care for yourself. You can refuse to react, and take to rest. You can guard your lonely heart (e.g., via inner bonding) and suppress your anger.

Sharing

Still another way to cope with stress and pain is to share. Instead of repressing our feelings, we can name and share them. We can share our thoughts and feelings with our self, others, and God.

Some people seek solitude to listen in silence. Others periodically go on retreats and keep a personal journal that facilitate self-awareness. Others share with a trustworthy and compassionate person.

PSYCHOLOGICAL STRATEGIES

The simple fact is that genuine listening and understanding invariably increase our well-being. When we can share our insides, we find that we decrease stress, conserve and increase energy, and basically cope better.

Ask trustworthy and caring persons to listen to you. If no one is available, you can seek a competent counselor or minister. It's also smart to join a fellowship where you will find people who have been where you are and who are trustworthy, understanding, and helpful.

You're mistaken if you feel that you're unique or that there are few people like you. There are many people who share your plight. When you share with people who really understand, who have more or less been where you are, you'll feel and be better.

You'll find that the boat you are on is far from empty, but that it's terribly crowded. Instead of feeling alien and alone, you realize that you are decidedly human and not alone.

Listen to this woman's account of her first S-Anon meeting. "Never in my wildest dreams did I think that so many people felt like I do. When I listened to them share, I thought they were talking about me. I just knew that they've been where I am, or at least in a similar situation.

"It helped to know that some of them were worse off than me and made it through in good shape. When I left the meeting, I felt that there was a way out of my mess, that somehow I'd make it. To say the least, it was, and still is, encouraging, hopeful, and inspiring."

However, not all people have such a positive experience at their initial meetings. Listen to this woman. "It took me months to get to an S-Anon meeting, and when I finally got to one, it didn't go very well. Yea, they were nice people, and definitely trustworthy. Their stories rang a few bells, but I felt that they were too different than mine.

"Only a couple of them had young children like me. Most of them were financially sound, at least that's the impression I got. Furthermore, the ones who seemed most settled were much older than I, and some of them stayed with their spouses. Those frames didn't seem to fit me.

"For some reason or other, I attended meetings, and I read some of their literature. It probably helped a little. I even got a sponsor, an older woman who helped me be kind to myself.

"Well, to abbreviate this story, I eventually realized that I was on the same boat as all of my S-Anon sisters, but in a different section. In time, I met a few women who were closer to my fourth class status. Their stories and situations were closer to mine. . I'm glad I kept going back, for the fellowship and its program helped to get back on my feet and stand up for myself."

Reach out. Seek help. Share with trustworthy and compassionate people. Connect and converse with your God and good people who can understand, console, and share with you. It would be a mistake not to do so.

When you bond in love with trustworthy others, you'll be strengthened, your burdens will lighten, your pain will lessen, and your nightmares will eventually change to good dreams. A miracle that makes everything right won't happen, but miracles will happen.

Humor

We usually think of humor when we are feeling good or when things are going well, but humor is also important when our life is going badly. Strange or mean-spirited as it may seem, humor can be helpful.

Humor helps us to de-stress, heal, and function more effectively. Smiling and laughing ease our grip on whatever bothers us as well as lessen our intensity and urgency to solve problems. When we pause, breathe, and smile, we are better off to think about the best course of action.

For instance, instead of raging or beating yourself when the abuser gets under skin, you can pause and internally smile. You can say to yourself, here I go again, needing or trying to change what I can't change. You can humbly admit that you fell into the same old trap, and kindly laugh at, with, and for yourself.

Your silent chuckle tells you that it's not the end of the world, that it's not a matter of all or nothing, and that you'll learn from your mistakes. Kind smiles and silent giggles are like comforting and encouraging pats of care.

Socially, humor is an equalizer. In genuine humor, we put aside our professional status, educational and cultural rank, and economic status in order to find and stand on common ground. In humor, we are not alone, but rather we connect with others.

It has been said that humor can be a springboard to the divine, opening us to more than is initially seen. Laughter and fun can give us a whisper of the sacred and a glimpse of what we all desire—to be in harmony with one another. In good humor, we feel more one with ourselves and others; we feel good.

So far, we have tried to understand and be compassionate with some of our problematic experiences. We have presented a psycho-spiritual paradigm as the basis of coping and healthy living. Our next task is to offer ways to communicate with the intimacy abuser.

Chapter Thirteen

Communication

INDEED, IT IS DAUNTING and frustrating to communicate with an abuser. What do you do, if he is unwilling or unable, for whatever reasons, to communicate honestly and openly? Let us reflect on what to avoid and what to do.

Listen to Lucy's communication comments. "God, I don't think there's anything more frustrating than when I try to have a decent conversation with him. I know that arguing invariably makes matters worse. He looks at me like I'm crazy, and he proclaims that he's not going to discuss anything with me as long as I'm so angry. And in some respects, he's right.

"However, I've improved. I've learned to stand up to him without arguing. No longer do I need him to say or act in the ways I like. In short, I stopped trying to make him be the way I'd like him to be.

"My dear manipulative husband was content when I said and did what he wanted. When he got his way, he was happy. In my co-dependent days, that is precisely what I'd do because when he was happy, I was happy. Happy!? Actually, I was enabling him and disabling myself.

Communication

"I've learned to set boundaries, as well as how to respond when he crosses them. I've learned to say no to him while saying yes to myself. I learned that my well-being comes from within me, not from him."

Through trail, error, and success, Lucy learned what did and did not work. She learned to avoid what made matters worse, and to practice what helped her. She learned to be aware of her needs and expectations, to set boundaries, to focus on issues, to control herself, and to deflect and detach from her husband's manipulation.

Like Lucy, avoid needing anything from a problematic person. Avoid needing him to hear and to understand you. Avoid expecting him to respect you, and to be honest and fair with you. Indeed, to "want" these kinds of behaviors is entirely legitimate, but to "need" is not.

Beware, however, that an abuser (or any addict) will at times meet your expectations and satisfy your needs, just enough to reinforce your neediness and expectations. He'll tell you what you want to hear. When he does communicate openly and fairly, hope that it happens the next time you talk, but don't expect it.

Sex abusers in real recovery communicate honestly and consistently. They won't fight or take flight, play blame games, change the subject, or overall be defensive. They'll listen and understand as well as show you respect. They'll also share their thoughts and feelings without trying to justify them or proving that they are the "right" ones.

Avoid arguing. You can ask yourself why you argue. Does he push your buttons? Are you trying to "make" him understand? Do you need to be right? Do you need to prove that you are smarter or healthier than he? Do you need him to see the light and to be decent?

Avoid needing and proving that you're right. When you're right and win, the other is wrong and loses, which usually incites the loser to be more defensive and combative. Putting the sex abuser or anyone down or in his place seldom does much good. Simply state what you think without proving your point—or, needing him to recognize or affirm your truth.

Avoid telling him what he should do. Avoid using phrases like "you need to" or "you better do this or else." You can state what you might do or what someone you know has done in a similar situation. But what he should do is his decision.

Whatever your motive, at best your fight will be a draw. You'll seldom win, and if you do win, you lose, for you are playing the same games as he does.

Avoid giving him a dose of his toxic medicine. Avoid criticizing, blaming, or shaming him to teach him a lesson. Avoid hurting him because he hurt you.

Being vindictive only evens the score at zero-zero. Submitting to and absorbing his abuse is even worse. Neither beat nor be beaten. Being a door mat or making him one only contributes to your misery.

Avoid shouting, threatening, and using foul language as well as pleading, pleasing, and diminishing. In doing so, you may gain some short-term relief, but long-term grief. Indeed, such behavior is understandable and terribly tempting, but it's not to be recommended. Instead, try to practice the following.

Don't be rushed; take your time (not his). If the offender (or anyone) pressures you to make a decision immediately, simply say that you'll think about the matter and get back to him at a later time. Then, you can reflect on the issue as well as consult with others.

Do give what you want to receive. Do listen and understand what the sexaholic is expressing. Do be silent, listen, and understand. Do reflect back to him what he's saying as you hear it. In other words, give what you want to receive.

Do let him be if he becomes defensive or contentious. Be calm rather than trying to make him be calm. If he blames you, simply say that you hear what he's saying, and you see it differently. If he insults you, tell him you know what and how he thinks and feels about you. If he continues to be abusive, leave the scene.

Do "share and check." Share a little, and check on his response. If he seems to be listening or at least trying to do so, you can share more. If he is argumentative or abusive, you can point that out. If he is unwilling or unable to hear you, then stop sharing. Share and check at another time. Don't try to "make" him listen.

Do use the word "I" and avoid using "you" as much as you can. Particularly in oppositional situations, "you" tends to be accusatory and connote judgment and blame, and often pressures and threatens a person. "I" statements are usually better than "you" statements.

When you say things like, "You scare me," "You broke my trust in you," "What's wrong with you," and "Won't you ever get it?", you are likely to put him on the defense where he fights or flights. Moreover, you inadvertently place the responsibility for how you feel on him.

A better way is to use "I", like "I get scared when . . .," "I can't trust when . . .," "I'm baffled with such behavior . . .," "I'm frustrated with . . ." Indeed, you include the behavior of the abuser in your statement, but you begin with yourself instead of him. Such an approach is far from guaranteed, but it's less likely to threaten and empower him, and more likely to empower and protect you.

Do take responsibility for how you feel rather than blaming him, even though he is a major cause. To wit, since you don't need (though want) him to co-operate and communicate, you are empowered.

If he needs to be right and attacks you, deflect his abuse, and point out his behavior. If he continues his self-righteous behavior, then stop, and try later.

To be sure, there are rights and wrongs, but it's usually unwise and nonproductive to force the issue. Rather than judging, lecturing, or arguing, it is invariably better to share your thoughts and feelings while checking his responses.

If you disagree with him, or you think he is grossly wrong, unfair, or delusional, say that you see things differently. Usually, it's better to focus on differences rather than rights and wrongs.

You might think that he's a dishonest, narcissistic, manipulative, and a pathetic piece of humanity. To tell him so, or lecture him on how sick, sinful, and criminal he is, will likely evoke an argument, withdrawal, or manipulative tears.

Do say something, just once, as clearly, calmly, and firmly as you can. If you say it twice, you're getting into trouble because you're probably trying to make him get it. If you repeat something three or more times, you're in trouble.

A saner and more effective approach is to listen to and reflect back what he is saying. Don't argue, prove him wrong, point out his fallacies, degrade or shame him. Do offer your views. Accurately repeat what the sexaholic is saying, demonstrating that you understand. Hopefully, your role-modeling encourages him to do the same, but don't bet on it.

When the abuser throws the discussion back on you with criticisms, blame, and other verbal attacks, you can bond within, and then deflect rather than absorb his comments. Instead of attacking back, you can firmly say that you see things differently. Instead of asking what's wrong with him, ask with compassion what has happened to him.

You neither condone nor condemn. You avoid fruitless arguments, and you hope, not expect, that you may have planted some seeds that may grow and bear fruit days or years later.

Chapter Fourteen

Forgiveness, Humility, and Gratitude

"It's been three years since we divorced. When I look back, I'm still horrified at how he jeopardized me and our children. I still get angry when I think about it. So much money spent on sex, and so many deceptions in service of his self-pleasure. Did he ever think of me and our children?

"It was all about him, and it's still that way. He still insists that his behavior is past, and we should focus on the present. He says that I should forgive and forget. God, do I resent him.

"Forgive? That'll be a cold day in hell. I'll never forgive him. Why should I? He ruined my life, and he continues to do so. We lost our house, and I'm still paying debts that I didn't incur. He pays very little child support, and often it's late. I get sick when I think about it.

"He's the same, tiresome Jeff who wants everything to go his way. It's all about him, never about us. Yet, the kids love dear old daddy, and seem to blame me that he's not around like he used to be. I deeply resent what he did to us. I'll never forgive him. Why should I?

"Yet, I have to admit that my bitterness is like a millstone around my neck. Meanwhile, he seems to be having a good old time without us. I'm miserable, and he seems happy. What should I do?"

Forgiveness

You probably feel for this woman. Not only did her husband demolish her trust and love, but he also put her and her children in serious jeopardy. Moreover, her ex-husband continues to be his narcissistic and manipulative self. Like her, why should you forgive someone who devastated your life?

Perhaps you've heard about people who have forgiven those who gravely hurt them. We may admire or be baffled by the mother who forgives her child's murderer, the husband who forgives the drunken driver who disabled his wife, the innocent prisoner who forgives his mistaken accusers, and the adult child who forgives her parents for their incestuous acts.

Indeed, such people are exceptional. They're not stupid, naïve, or insane, but rather they're smart, wise, and sane. Forgiveness is one of the most difficult virtues to practice, yet it's important for your well-being. Part of the difficulty is our misconceptions about what true forgiveness really is.

That being said, to forgive and forget is often a mistake. This is exactly what many abusers want you to do, namely forget about it and get on with life. Indeed, you should get on with life, but you remember (not obsess) and learn from the past.

Remember the devastation and pain so that you don't slip into past patterns of co-dependency. More so, remember so that you don't hurt again. Remembering helps you to protect yourself so that what did happen will not happen again.

Remembering what he did can help you to be on guard, to set boundaries, and to take care of yourself. You resent being abused. Such "good resentment" is a warning that the abuser better not mess with you again.

However, we seldom look at resentment in this positive light, and for good reasons, for resentment is often negative and destructive. Negative resentment means we obsess about the negative and need justice. We drink our own poison and expect the abuser to suffer.

We get caught in the lethal trap of resentment when we need what we won't get—justice, understanding, apologies, and amends. We fall back into the quicksand of co-dependency, looking for our well-being outside our self, and being resentful when it doesn't happen.

Thus, avoid reinforcing and acting on such resentment. Using spiritual and psychological resources, we can bond within, suppress, and detach from resentful thoughts and feelings. We can realize that holding grudges and needing justice will hurt us.

To be sure, this doesn't mean that you condone, minimize, rationalize, excuse, or forget what happened. Forgiveness doesn't mean that you whitewash the dark side of your life, but you do shed light on it.

When we forgive, we love—sinners and saints, criminals and law abiders, sick and healthy, insane and sane, addicts and co-addicts, forgotten and remembered, disabled and abled, disliked and liked, seemingly unlovable and loveable. We strive to give the mercy of forgiveness because there is no better way. Love calls us to forgive.

Like the biblical parent of the prodigal child, we prudently and patiently wait to see if the abuser is genuinely in recovery, has turned his life around, or has had a conversion. We're not foolish; we wait and see. And if he or she never appears on the horizon of humility and contrition, we let go and let God. We forgive.

Don't forget yourself. While the sexaholic is the perpetrator, you probably need to forgive yourself. You may have to forgive yourself for enabling the sexaholic, for blindly trusting him, for making him better than you, for satisfying his needs at your expense, for letting him abuse you, and for abusing yourself.

Maybe you forgive yourself for being vindictive, for drinking too much or for abusing other drugs, for eating or sleeping too much or too little, for sexual promiscuity, for poor work performance, for mean behavior, or simply for disappearing. Beware, co-dependency makes it easier to forgive others than to forgive yourself.

When you forgive yourself, you stop beating, blaming, and demeaning yourself, and you embrace yourself with merciful love. You smile with compassion at your well-intentioned mistakes. With unconditional love, you heal your wounds and learn new ways to love. After all, love is for imperfect people.

Forgiving yourself and others brings consolation and reconciliation, severing the chains of unhealthy resentment and its poisonous effects. Although forgiveness doesn't wipe the slate clean, it does enable you to live effectively and serenely with a smudged slate.

Humility and Gratitude

Humility and gratitude are also crucial for your survival and growth. It may seem cruel and nonsensical to encourage you to be humble and grateful, for these very qualities, albeit in their co-dependent forms, may have contributed to your troubles.

For instance, out of false humility, you may have submitted to satisfy the abuser's needs, bowed to his delusional superiority, and enabled him to do what he wanted. You may have played the humble, suffering servant. Now, you may feel sick and tired of being "humble" in putting up with his narcissism.

What do you have to be grateful for? Should you be grateful for being betrayed and violated? Should you be grateful for being demeaned, dishonored, and exploited? Should you be grateful for being humiliated? Indeed, no! Let's take a closer look at healthy humility and gratitude, and why they are important.

First of all, humility is not the same as humiliation. Although they both have the same Latin derivation, *humus* = earth, they are quite different. Humility is when we know our place on earth, and humiliation is when someone rubs your face in mud.

Forgiveness, Humility, and Gratitude

When we're humiliated, we're degraded, deceived, demeaned, dismissed, and diminished. We're put down and treated as being significantly less than we really are. When humiliation gives birth to shame, we want to hide and disappear.

Never allow anyone, including yourself, to dishonor you. Don't expose yourself to insult and abuse. Not only does humiliation hurt and weaken you, it empowers the abuser.

However, it may be tempting to practice what you hate. You can look at the sexaholic like he's garbage, relentlessly tell him how despicable he is, and work on scandalizing his name. Understandable, but not good. This doesn't mean that you should cover and lie for him, or pretend that everything is alright. You can tell the truth and share what you think is appropriate.

Humility means that you are powerless over the sexaholic, that is, you have less power than you think or would like to have. You recognize and accept your limits, like you cannot change or fix him. Humility, however, does not mean that you are helpless; in fact, true humility empowers you.

When you are humble, you admit that you are not the center of the universe, or the greatest power, or God. You know your place on earth, and are thankfully dependent on a greater reality than yourself. Contrary to exhibiting pride, you rely on others and God, not simply on yourself.

When we accept that we are power-less, we can connect with our Greater Power and become more power-full. Being down to earth can move us to look up, out, and within to the power of Love,

When you and I humbly admit to our shortcomings, new possibilities open up. Our limits can lead us to the unlimited, powerlessness to power, despair to hope, and death to life. Believe it or not, we can come to a new and deeper order, freedom, and peace. We can be grateful.

Feel Debbie's feelings. "Grateful? I should be grateful? What do I have to be grateful for? I bore and raised our children while he was whoring around. He screwed me, while screwing others. You can say I've been royally screwed my entire marriage. Grateful? For what?

"I think it's cruel to imply that I should be grateful. I worked myself almost to death in taking care of my kids and home. I worked outside our house to keep our financial heads above water. I swallowed my pride, and humbly accepted my bed of nails. I loved, supported, and trusted a man who was unfaithful with many women. How humiliating!"

Humiliating, indeed. No person should be grateful for being humiliated and betrayed. You should resent such behavior, and at the same time avoid getting stuck in negative resentment. How can Debbie, and you, be grateful?

A mystic once said that if you could say only one prayer, it would be two words: "Thank You."

Why is gratitude so important? The etymology of gratitude can give us a hint, for the Latin *gratia* means both thanks and grace. When we practice gratitude, we connect, at least implicitly, with our Higher Power.

In general, gratitude invites us to pause and look for the good. When you practice gratitude, you lighten up and see more. Gratitude simply makes you feel better.

Being thankful broadens our perspective, helps us see the negative in light of the positive, brings balance to our outlook, and combats getting stuck in the mire of resentment and depression. When you feel you are drowning in a flood of negativity, gratitude can rescue you.

To say "thank you" (for people, nature, animals, beauty, truth, love, life, God . . .) is sobering, consoling, and liberating. Even if you feel there is little positive in your life, you are alive, and life awaits you. What greater gift is there than life?

It is wise to practice an attitude of gratitude. Every day, you can think of five or more things to be grateful for. In the midst of "no's," you whisper a grateful "yes!" Perhaps with tears, you smile. Gratitude is saying yes!

Chapter Fifteen

New Life

THROUGHOUT THIS BOOK, WE have promised that your life can become better than ever. Initially, such a promise may have sounded impossible or unrealistic; hopefully, it is beginning to sound possible and doable.

My intent has been to assure you that your suffering is not futile but rather can lead you to a better life. I want your pain to count for something positive.

To be sure, especially in the early stages of recovery, such a process in which the positive and healthy triumph over the negative and unhealthy is easier said than done. Indeed, progress is likely to include some slips and relapses—but even they can help you.

Slips and Relapses

Whether you are new or an old-timer in recovery, you can probably sympathize with Lillian. "I know I'm not an old-timer, but I have been working the S-Anon diligently for a good fifteen months. Believe me. The fellowship and my Higher Power saved my sanity, and I'm grateful. I've come a long way.

"I no longer let my sexaholic husband push my buttons. I've learned to protect myself, set boundaries, and detach. And I continue to learn how to keep my freedom and serenity no matter what.

"So, what am I upset about? Well, the last two months have been horrible. Lately, I feel as though I'm back at square one, starting all over again. In my more rational moments, I know this is not true; nevertheless, I don't feel good. It's as if I'm my old, miserable co-dependent self. It's as if I've forgotten most of what I learned. My pink cloud has turned to dark purple.

"Like in the old days of misery, I find myself needing him to be a certain way, and trying to steer him in that direction. I catch myself starting to argue, to threaten divorce, to expos his sordid story.

"Still, I'm aware of my insane behavior, and I guess that's sane. I do try to curb and stop my futile efforts to control and hurt him. However, the battle continues in my mind—why did he do this to me and the children? He still doesn't get it. How can I make him hurt as much as I did?

"Yes, I tell myself, he has a disease. Then I say, baloney, he's a selfish, narcissistic creep. These kinds of thoughts run rampant through my mind, and of course, cause havoc with my serenity. My sponsor tells me that I'm having a relapse.

"It helps me when my S-Anon members share their slips and relapses, and what they did to get out of them. They even say that they learned from and grew stronger through them. That's hard to believe, but I trust them. They tell me that if I work the program, I'll come out of my insanity for the better."

Listen to Margie, Lillian's sponsor. "It hurts when I listen to Lillian's old demons luring her into a dark hole of miserable confinement. It hurts to see her regress to negative thinking and behaviors, but she knows more than she thinks she knows. I believe in her, and trust that she'll come out of this as a better person.

"With a compassionate smile, others and I share our relapses and slips, how we felt about the stupid and insane things that we did after years of acting sane. We tell her that she'll get off this merry-go-round. At least, this is what happened to us. As we say, we share our experience, strength, and hope.

"One of the stories I shared was how I slipped into old futile thinking and behavior. Those ten hours felt like ten years. During my brief descent into hell, I found myself stuck in the morass of trying to control what I couldn't control. You see, I caught him looking at raunchy porn again, though he said that was the first time in more than a dozen years. How could I believe him?

"Although I knew better, my feelings and mind kept saying that I can't trust him. His change was a sham, and he'll never be the man that I thought he was. I was fed up with accepting what I cannot change. Screw acceptance; now I'll declare war, and give him a taste of his own medicine. I'll give him more than a piece of my mind.

"Well, I could hear my sponsor say inside me that if maiming, torturing, or killing him would help, she'd support me. But I know that it would just make things worse—and, it wouldn't solve the problem.

"With the grace of God, I came to admit that the problem was in me, and that's good because that's something I could change. I smiled at myself on my knees, and I got up, looked up, and walked forward again.

"I humbly realized that I'm a human being who slipped into an old but familiar pattern of co-dependent thinking and behavior. And, maybe my husband had a slip. Indeed, my slip has helped me grow stronger. My prideful self was humbled, and I am grateful."

Lillian and Margie are examples of a relapse and a slip. Margie, the old-timer, humbly admits that she slipped or regressed to old behavior for a while. Old demons surfaced to taunt and lure her into futility. When she humbly admitted her shortcoming of pride (she could change her husband, she was too good for such injustice, etc.), she came out of her hell with a humble and confident smile.

We can see that a "slip" refers to a relatively brief regression to past thinking and behavior that make matters worse. As Margie indicated, negative behavior will dissipate in time, though it seldom disappears permanently. In a sense, our demons come and go, but seldom die.

Think of events that can trigger futile thoughts, feelings, and behaviors. For instance, you may be watching television with your recovering spouse, and you think he's lusting after a scantily clad woman. Immediately, you react with anxious and angry feelings. Or, you see the car of your ex-spouse in front of a porn shop, and you react with fury.

When you, like Lillian, get stuck in such thoughts or behaviors, be kind and gentle with yourself. Don't engage in catastrophic thinking; that is, don't make a mountain out of a mole hill. Avoid guilt and self-punishment. Humbly smile. Practice HABITS and cope. Treat yourself as well as you would treat your best friend.

Slips are relatively frequent and brief, while relapses happen less and last longer. The good news is that they can help us in our recovery. When we face, learn from, and cope with our weakness, we invariably become stronger.

From a Jungian perspective, when we face and re-channel the forces of our dark, shadow self, we mature (individuate) and become more enlightened. Indeed, when we walk through the valley of death, we gain new life.

Although most people in recovery will have tiny slips or temptations, they are unlikely to have extended relapses. Nevertheless, some after many years of healthy living, relapse.

A not uncommon reason is that we become lax in working a good program. Perhaps out of pride (I don't need help any more), or simply out of forgetfulness (due to busyness or stress), old demons lure us back to hell. Thus, it behooves us to be humble and vigilant.

Renewal

Our goal is to make our breakdown be a breakthrough to a better life. Rather than getting stuck in bad habits and bitterness, our challenge is to come to good habits and peace.

Rather than living a broken life, our wounds can heal, and our psychological and spiritual scars can make us stronger. Again, these promises are realistic, and they can come true.

In the beginning of this book, we talked about how you were and will be dissed—disillusioned, dismissed, discombobulated, disrupted, disgraced, disputed, displaced, disjointed, disregarded, and on and on. A recurrent theme has been how you can transform your deficits and vices into assets and virtues.

Instead of getting stuck in the mire of being dissed, you can transform your life. One way of framing this process of self-renewal is that you can move from being "dissed" to being "re-ed." You can add your own "re" words to the following list.

Now you can seize the opportunities to renew, recuperate, recover, rebound, reform, restore, regain, repair, redo, recover, reclaim, remember, review, recollect, reorder, rebuild, regulate, reorient, reclaim, rectify, retrieve, retreat, recharge, reinforce, retool, refuse, reject, renounce, resist, revolt, reverse, reconcile, return, respond, reconnect, relate, respect, redeem, rejuvenate, regenerate, revivify, rekindle, recreate, relax, rejoice, and on and on.

A "re" word indicates that we go back to look at things differently in order to improve our life. In psychological parlance, we practice cognitive restructuring. Actually, our life can become a continuous re-new-al.

For instance, you refuse to fall apart, roll over, give up, or become dysfunctional, and you resist the temptation to numb your pain with alcohol, sex, or other temporary satisfactions. Likewise, you refuse to fight the abuser, and you reject and renounce his manipulative games.

You recover from your desolation and disillusionment by grieving your losses, retooling with new and effective strategies, and rekindling your spirit. You remember and recollect what has happened so that you learn from your experience. You revolt by changing yourself, not him.

You retrieve and recharge your healthy self as well as reconnect and relate with healthy people. Moreover, you rejuvenate yourself with relaxation, recreation, and other regenerating activities.

Most importantly, you reorient and reorder your life by drawing on your resources, primarily love for and from self, others, and God. You reconcile with yourself and God and as well as you can with others. Consequently, you rejoice, for your life has been and will continue to be renewed.

These are not foolhardy promises. They can and will come true. With trust and hope, you can and will be freer, stronger, and happier. You can and will mitigate your pain. You can and will heal and renew your life. You can and will live serenely in Love.

Chapter Sixteen

A Postscript to Sex Abusers

IN THIS BOOK, I have been a defender of and for people who trusted and loved a sex/intimacy abuser. My goal has been to recognize and give unintended victims a voice and to help them cope, heal, and grow.

To pursue this goal, I may have seemed harsh to sex abusers. However, what I have offered victims may help you, a sex abuser, and your enablers as well. If you are a sex/intimacy abuser (or an enabler) who wants to be healthy and make amends, start with yourself. Let me speak to you.

You cannot expect people to understand or be compassionate with you. Sex abusers, especially those who engaged minors or were physically violent, are treated as the lowest of social and criminal offenders. Moreover, few people will grasp how the magnetic force and slippery slope of sex abuse can seduce you, how it lures you into a make-believe world of power and pleasure.

Your intent was probably not to abuse, betray, or violate your loved ones; unless you are a perpetrator of incest, you may not have given it much thought. When you enter the worlds of lustful sex, you repress or forget about your loved ones, for they could get you to think and feel differently.

Thus, if you want to get healthy, keep your loved ones and God in the picture at all times; after all, you say that you care about them. When lust lures you, remember your loved ones.

You can also practice good HABITS, avoid people, places, and things that trigger your disorder—and, abstain from or suppress any lustful thoughts, feelings, and behaviors.

You can humbly surrender to a Higher Power that can help you gain the courage to change. Don't isolate; do reach out to people who can help you. Don't be self-sufficient; do connect with your Higher Power. Don't be narcissistic; do accept, understand, and care for others.

Don't blame; do take responsibility for your recovery. Don't make excuses; do be contrite, ask for forgiveness, and make amends. Don't despair; do hope that you will become the person you are meant to be.

Keep in mind that health and lust, as we have defined them, are mutually exclusive. You must learn to see others with eyes of love, not lust. Moreover, you must consistently perceive not only a person's body but also his or her personality and spirit. Clearly, you hurt yourself and others when you forget or reject the whole person.

To make amends, leave your narcissistic world and enter your loved ones' worlds. Enter their desolation and disillusionment. Humbly accept their rage, doubts, criticisms, and contempt. Feel their pain, experience their betrayal, listen to their anger, and weep with them. One day at a time, walk this talk of reform, recovery, and reconciliation

In conversations, don't criticize, blame, make excuses, or change the subject, but rather accept, understand, listen, and truly care without strings attached. In everyday living, be honest, responsible, and helpful with finances, chores, and personal issues. Avoid forcing anything, but be available. Make your own list of the qualities and behaviors of a contrite and good person.

A Postscript to Sex Abusers

Changes of heart, mind, and behavior are difficult. Many of you can recover, but not alone. Seek help, like twelve step programs or competent counselors, or both.

Remember, you got away with your unhealthy behavior probably for a long time. You had to sneak, hide, lie, cover, manipulate, exploit, and violate others to achieve your goals of power and pleasure. It takes commitment and work to break your bad habits and to replace them with healthy ones.

Although abstinence is the first of many steps on the road to recovery, in itself it is not enough. You must also change the way you look at and live life. Moreover, if you only use will power to stop acting on your lust, you'll be left with a vacuum that will demand fulfillment.

You must fill the hole in your soul with healthy activities; otherwise, you'll slip and relapse again and again. Your life, not just your sexuality, has to change in ways that are healthy for you and others.

Becoming healthy is no guarantee that you and your loved ones will reconcile. Moreover, you will fail if you try to change only to please your spouse, for again you are manipulating her.

Question yourself. Regardless of what happens, can my crimes move me to be an honorable man? Can my narcissism challenge me to care for others? Can my dishonesty and lies lead to honesty and truth? Can my isolation pressure me to foster fellowship? Can my sickness spur me to health?

Can my vices convert to virtues? Can my bad behavior inspire me to be good? Can my shame and guilt lead to worth and freedom? Can my doubts evoke faith? Can my despair engender hope? Can my lust transform to love? Some can and do turn their lives around. Will you?

Bibliography

Adams, Christine A. *Love, Infidelity, and Sexual Addiction. Codependent's Perspective.* San Jose, CA: Authors Choice, 2000.

Blume, Sue E. *Secret Survivors. Uncovering Incest and Its Aftereffects in Women.* NY: Ballantine Books, 1990.

Carnes, Patrick. Out of the Shadows. *Understanding Sexual Addictions.* Center City, MN: Hazelden, 2001.

Carnes, Stefanie, ed. *Mending Shattered Hearts. A Guide for Partners of Sex Addicts.* Carefree, AZ: Gentle Path, 2011.

Carnes, Stefanie and Anthony D. Rodriguez. *Facing Heartbreak. Steps to Recovery for Partners of Sex Addicts.* Carefree. AZ: 2012

Corley, M. Deborah and Jennifer Schneider. *Surviving Disclosure: A Partner's Guide for Healing the Betrayal of Intimate Trust.* Tucson AZ: Recovery Resources, 2012.

Crosson-Tower, Cynthia. *A Clergy Guide to Child Abuse and Neglect.* Cleveland, OH: Pilgrim, 2000.

Daily Readings for Anyone Affected by Another Person's Sexual Behavior. Reflections of Hope. Nashville, TN: S-Anon International Family Groups, 2008.

Dawson, Emma. *My Secret Life with a Sex Addict. From Discovery to Recovery.* Parker, CO: Thornton, 2005.

Desk Reference to the Diagnostic Criteria from DSM-5. Washington, D.C.: America Psychiatric Association, 2013.

Gallagher, Kathy. *When His Secret Sin Breaks Your Heart.* Dry Ridge, KY: Pure Life Ministries, 2003.

Kraft, William F. *Coming to God.* Eugene, OR: Wipf and Stock, 2015.

———. *Sexuality and Spirituality, Pursuing Integration.* Eugene, OR: Wipf and Stock, 2005.

———. *When You Care about a Functional Alcoholic.* Mahwah, NJ. Paulist, 2011.

BIBLIOGRAPHY

Lassar, Debra. *Shattered Vows. Hope and Healing for Women Who Have Been Betrayed.* Grand Rapids, MI: Zondervan, 2008.

O'Murchu, Diarmuid. Quantum Theology. *Spiritual Implications of the New Physics.* NY: Crossroads, 2004.

S-Anon Twelve Steps. Nashville, TN: S-Anon International Family Groups, 2000.

Sex and Love Addicts Anonymous. Norwood, MA: The Augustine Fellowship, 1986.

Sexaholics Anonymous. Simi Valley, CA: SA Literature, 1989.

Schneider, Jennifer. *Sex, Lies, and Forgiveness.* Tucson, AZ: Recovery Resources, 1999.

Steffens, Barbara and Marsha Means. *Sexually Addicted Spouse. How Partners Can Cope and Heal.* Far Hills, NJ: New Horizon, 2009.

Stoeker, Fred and Brenda. *Every Heart Restored. A Wife's Guide to Healing in the Wake of a Husband's Sexual Sin.* Colorado Springs, CO: Waterbrook, 2004.

Wilson, Meg. *Hope after Betrayal. Healing When Sexual Addiction Invades Your Marriage.* Grand Rapids, MI: Kregel Publications, 2007.

www.ingramcontent.com/pod-product-compliance
Lightning Source LLC
Chambersburg PA
CBHW070933160426
43193CB00011B/1674